FREEDOM FROM CRUEL AND UNUSUAL PUNISHMENT

Edited by Kristin O'Donnell Tubb

Bruce Glassman, *Vice President*
Bonnie Szumski, *Publisher*
Helen Cothran, *Managing Editor*
Scott Barbour, *Series Editor*

GREENHAVEN PRESS
An imprint of Thomson Gale, a part of The Thomson Corporation

Detroit • New York • San Francisco • San Diego • New Haven, Conn.
Waterville, Maine • London • Munich

THOMSON

GALE

LIBRARY OF CONGRESS CATALOGING-IN-PUBLICATION DATA

Freedom from cruel and unusual punishment / Kristin O'Donnell Tubb, book editor.
    p. cm. — (The Bill of Rights)
Includes bibliographical references and index.
ISBN 0-7377-1925-7 (lib. : alk. paper)
    1. Punishment—United States. I. Tubb, Kristin O'Donnell. II. The Bill of Rights (San Diego, Calif.)

KF9225.F74 2005
345.73'077—dc22   2004054223

Printed in the United States of America

The Bill of Rights

CONTENTS

Chapter 1: Early History of Prohibiting Cruel and Unusual Punishment

1. A Bill of Rights Is Needed to Prevent Cruel and Unusual Punishment

One of the most vociferous proponents of the Bill of Rights discusses the importance of limiting the power of Congress through a clause prohibiting cruel and unusual punishments.

2. The Founders Included the Eighth Amendment to Prohibit Torture

Under English law, the phrase *cruel and unusual* meant "excessive." The founders misinterpreted the phrase to mean "punishment using torturous methods."

3. The Supreme Court Expands the Definition of Cruel and Unusual Punishment

The Supreme Court in *Weems v. United States* (1910) ruled that the Eighth Amendment applied not only to punishments considered cruel and unusual by the framers in 1789 but also to punishments considered cruel and unusual according to society's evolving standards.

Chapter 2: The Eighth Amendment and the Death Penalty

Chapter 3: What Forms of Punishment Are Cruel and Unusual?

"I cannot agree with those who think of the Bill of Rights as an 18th Century straightjacket, unsuited for this age. . . . The evils it guards against are not only old, they are with us now, they exist today."

—Hugo Black, associate justice of the
U.S. Supreme Court, 1937–1971

The Bill of Rights codifies the freedoms most essential to American democracy. Freedom of speech, freedom of religion, the right to bear arms, the right to a trial by a jury of one's peers, the right to be free from cruel and unusual punishment—these are just a few of the liberties that the Founding Fathers thought it necessary to spell out in the first ten amendments to the U.S. Constitution.

While the document itself is quite short (consisting of fewer than five hundred words), and while the liberties it protects often seem straightforward, the Bill of Rights has been a source of debate ever since its creation. Throughout American history, the rights the document protects have been tested and reinterpreted. Again and again, individuals perceiving violations of their rights have sought redress in the courts. The courts in turn have struggled to decipher the original intent of the founders as well as the need to accommodate changing societal norms and values.

The ultimate responsibility for addressing these claims has fallen to the U.S. Supreme Court. As the highest court in the nation, it is the Supreme Court's role to interpret the Constitution. The Court has considered numerous cases in which people have accused government of impinging on their rights. In the process, the Court has established a body of case law and precedents that have, in a sense, defined the Bill of Rights. In doing so, the Court has often reversed itself and introduced new ideas and approaches that have altered the legal meaning of the rights contained in the Bill of Rights. As a general rule, the Court has erred on the side of caution, upholding and expanding the rights of individuals rather than restricting them.

An example of this trend is the definition of cruel and unusual punishment. The Eighth Amendment specifically states, "Excessive bail shall not be required, nor excessive fines imposed, nor cruel and unusual punishments inflicted." However, over the years the Court has had to grapple with defining what constitutes "cruel and unusual punishment." In colonial America, punishments for crimes included branding, the lopping off of ears, and whipping. Indeed, these punishments were considered lawful at the time the Bill of Rights was written. Obviously, none of these punishments are legal today. In order to justify outlawing certain types of punishment that are deemed repugnant by the majority of citizens, the Court has ruled that it must consider the prevailing opinion of the masses when making such decisions. In overturning the punishment of a man stripped of his citizenship, the Court stated in 1958 that it must rely on society's "evolving standards of decency" when determining what constitutes cruel and unusual punishment. Thus the definition of cruel and unusual is not frozen to include only the types of punishment that were illegal at the time of the framing of the Bill of Rights; specific modes of punishment can be rejected as society deems them unjust.

Another way that the Courts have interpreted the Bill of Rights to expand individual liberties is through the process of "incorporation." Prior to the passage of the Fourteenth Amendment, the Bill of Rights was thought to prevent only the federal government from infringing on the rights listed in the document. However, the Fourteenth Amendment, which was passed in the wake of the Civil War, includes the words, ". . . nor shall any state deprive any person of life, liberty, or property, without due process of law; nor deny to any person within its jurisdiction the equal protection of the laws." Citing this passage, the Court has ruled that many of the liberties contained in the Bill of Rights apply to state and local governments as well as the federal government. This process of incorporation laid the legal foundation for the civil rights movement—most specifically the 1954 *Brown v. Board of Education* ruling that put an end to legalized segregation.

As these examples reveal, the Bill of Rights is not static. It truly is a living document that is constantly being reinterpreted and redefined. The Bill of Rights series captures this vital aspect of one of America's most cherished founding texts. Each volume in the series focuses on one particular right protected in the Bill of Rights. Through the use of primary and secondary sources, the right's evolution is traced from colonial times to the present. Primary sources include landmark Supreme Court rulings, speeches by prominent experts, and editorials. Secondary sources include historical analyses, law journal articles, book excerpts, and magazine articles. Each book also includes several features to facilitate research, including a bibliography, an annotated table of contents, an annotated list of relevant Supreme Court cases, an introduction, and an index. These elements help to make the Bill of Rights series a fascinating and useful tool for examining the fundamental liberties of American democracy.

"Excessive bail shall not be required, nor excessive fines imposed, nor cruel and unusual punishments inflicted."
—The Eighth Amendment to the United States Constitution

"Without the Eighth Amendment, the U.S. would be just another police state, governed by fear."
—Coretta Scott King[1]

Power is a mysterious force, so ingrained in human nature that the tradition of Judeo-Christian ethics recounts the struggle to acquire it as man's first act of defiance: Eve plucks an apple from a tree in order to gain the power of knowledge. Many ethicists interpret this urge for power as man's original sin.

The very definition of power necessitates that one party dominate another. Yet in the United States this notion must coexist with the ideals of a democracy, a state in which each person is considered free and equal. While the struggle for power is omnipresent ("All the world is in pursuit of power,"[2] says poet-philosopher Ralph Waldo Emerson), a true democracy finds ways to limit power. In fact, the very heart of democracy is finding a fair distribution of power. "The nation which will not adopt an equilibrium of power," said founding father John Adams, "must adopt a despotism. There is no other alternative."[3]

Residing at opposite ends of the ideological spectrum, democracy and despotism—or authoritarianism—do have one commonality: Their very essence is defined by how much power the ruling class possesses. As a democracy strives to limit and balance power between leaders and citizens, an authoritarian state is characterized by absolute compliance with authority. "The doctrine of blind obedience and unqualified submission to any human power, whether civil or ecclesiastical, is the doctrine of despotism,"[4] wrote abolitionist Angela Grimké in the *Anti-Slavery Examiner* in 1836.

Power manifests itself in many forms: control over natural resources like oil and water; the esteem placed on powerful positions in society, such as the roles of police officer and judge; the ability to direct the dissemination of information. Yet possibly the most basic form of power is the ability to punish others.

Having the power to punish is a heady responsibility, one that allows the empowered to sculpt the behavior of the powerless. "In its function, the power to punish is not essentially different from curing or educating,"[5] says French philosopher Michel Foucault. As such, the power to punish can easily be abused. Indeed, some theorists believe that punishment may exist for the sole purpose of reinforcing existing positions of power. According to renowned German philosopher Friedrich Nietzsche, "The purpose of punishment is to improve those who do the punishing—that is the final recourse of those who support punishment."[6]

Limiting the Ability to Punish

If a democracy requires the balancing of power, and one of the most basic forms of power is the ability to punish, then a democratic state must limit the ability to punish. This fact became painfully evident to the group of citizens who endured the "Reign of Terror" in seventeenth-century England. During this era the monarchy ruled England by using such terrifying tactics as drawing and quartering for offenses that equaled the modern-day version of passing a bad check. When the rulers were overthrown and a more democratic state was formed, the English Bill of Rights of 1689 limited the types of punishments allowed with a clause that stated, "excessive bail ought not to be required, nor excessive fines imposed, nor cruel and unusual punishments inflicted."[7]

America's founding fathers also believed in this tenet to such an extent that the Eighth Amendment was almost omitted because it was deemed too commonsensical. Yet some critics of the Constitution feared that if the document lacked such a provision, Congress would wield too much power to punish. As stated by Patrick Henry,

Congress, from their general powers, may fully go into business of human legislation. They may legislate, in criminal cases, from treason to the lowest offence—petty larceny. They may define crimes and prescribe punishments. In the definition of crimes, I trust they will be directed by what wise representatives ought to be governed by. But when we come to punishments, no latitude ought to be left, nor dependence put on the virtue of representatives.[8]

Due to the concerns expressed by Henry and other founders, the amendment was included in the Bill of Rights, in a form that all but plagiarizes the 1689 English Bill of Rights.

Most people agree that government must be limited in its power to punish. However, debate has emerged over the definition of "cruel and unusual." It was easy for the constitutional framers to foresee that this wording would be the crux of future disputes. Melancton Smith of South Carolina objected to "the import of [the words] being too indefinite," while Samuel Livermore stated, "What is meant by the terms excessive bail? Who are to be the judges? What is understood by excessive fines? . . . [I]t is sometimes necessary to hang a man, villains often deserve whipping, and perhaps having their ears cut off; but are we in the future to be prevented from inflicting these punishments because they are cruel?"[9]

The types of punishment that are deemed cruel and unusual have changed over the years. For example, as the Livermore quote suggests, whipping and cutting of ears were once considered acceptable punishments in the United States. These methods of punishment have long fallen out of favor. In rejecting certain punishments as excessive, the Supreme Court has stated that the Eighth Amendment was intended to evolve along with society's changing standards regarding the acceptable treatment of criminals

The Death Penalty

Not surprisingly, most Eighth Amendment debate currently centers on capital punishment—the death penalty and how it is imposed. The Supreme Court has had difficulty remaining consistent in translating this troublesome clause when it comes to the imposition of death. In 1972 the Court declared: "Death sentences are cruel and unusual in the same way that being struck by lightning is cruel and unusual."[10] Yet just four years later, that same Court said, "Death is an extreme sanction, suitable to the most extreme of crimes."[11] Regardless of the Court's imprimatur, debate continues over the constitutionality of this ultimate punishment.

Despite the problematic wording of the amendment and its ever-evolving nature, its presence is necessary to restrict those who have been placed in positions of power. Perhaps the vague wording is also a blessing, allowing flexibility in its application. After all, the Supreme Court itself has recognized that what might be considered perfectly acceptable today may be cruel and unusual tomorrow. But one thing is certain: An absence of this amendment could lead to an abuse of power and perhaps a bloody rebellion against that abuse. It is a specific check on the power bestowed upon America's leaders, thereby distinguishing the government of the United States as a true democracy.

Notes

1. Quoted in Linda R. Monk, *The Words We Live By: Your Annotated Guide to the Constitution*. New York: Stonesong/Hyperion, 2003, p. 184.
2. Ralph Waldo Emerson, "Culture," essay in *The Conduct of Life*. Boston: Houghton Mifflin, 1896.
3. Quoted in C. Wright Mills, *The Power Elite*. New York: Oxford University Press, 2002, p. 242.
4. Angela Grimké, "Appeal to the Christian Women of the South," *Anti-Slavery Examiner*, September 1836, reprinted in *The Oven Birds: American Women on Womanhood, 1820–1920*. Ed. Gail Parker. Garden City, NY: Anchor, 1972.
5. Michel Foucault, *Discipline and Punish: The Birth of the Prison*. Trans. Alan Sheridan. New York: Pantheon, 1975.
6. Friedrich Nietzsche, *Sämtliche Werke: Kritische Studienausgabe*. Vol. 3. New York: De Gruyter, 1980, p. 509.
7. Quoted in *Furman v. Georgia*, 1972, p. 4.
8. Quoted in Jonathan Elliot, *The Debates in the Several State Conventions on the Adoption of the Constitution*. 2nd ed. Vol. 3. New York: Burt Franklin, 1888, pp. 447–48.
9. Quoted in *Weems v. United States*, 1910.
10. *Furman v. Georgia*, 1972, p. 34.
11. *Gregg v. Georgia*, 1976, p. 23.

Early History of Prohibiting Cruel and Unusual Punishment

The Bill of Rights

A Bill of Rights Is Needed to Prevent Cruel and Unusual Punishment

Patrick Henry

Upon the completion of the initial draft of the U.S. Constitution in 1787, delegates returned home to their respective states; each state then held a convention to discuss whether to adopt this new governmental framework. The largest point of contention at these state conventions was that the document lacked a bill of rights securing individual freedoms. Many states refused to ratify the Constitution without the inclusion of a bill of rights. During the Convention of the Commonwealth of Virginia, Patrick Henry discussed the importance of limiting the power of Congress by including a bill of rights, specifically a clause prohibiting cruel and unusual punishments. Without such a clause, he purported, Congress would have full control to prescribe any number of punishments for even the pettiest of crimes—an amount of power "extremely dangerous to liberty." Obviously, the arguments of Henry and others struck a nerve, as the Constitution was amended with the Bill of Rights that includes a clause restricting punishments. Patrick Henry is one of the most well-known participants in the struggle for American liberty. This three-time governor of Virginia is perhaps best remembered for his famous "Give me liberty or give me death!" speech less than one month before the start of the American Revolutionary War.

Without a bill of rights, you will exhibit the most absurd thing to mankind that ever the world saw—a government

Patrick Henry, speech before the Convention of the Commonwealth of Virginia, June 16, 1788.

that has abandoned all its powers—the powers of direct taxation, the sword, and the purse. You have disposed of them to Congress, without a bill of rights—without check, limitation, or control. And still you have checks and guards; still you keep barriers—pointed where? Pointed against your weakened, prostrated, enervated state government! You have a bill of rights to defend you against the state government, which is bereaved of all power, and yet you have none against Congress, though in full and exclusive possession of all power! You arm yourselves against the weak and defenceless, and expose yourselves naked to the armed and powerful. Is not this a conduct of unexampled absurdity? What barriers have you to oppose to this most strong, energetic government? To that government you have nothing to oppose. All your defence is given up. This is a real, actual defect. It must strike the mind of every gentleman. When our government was first instituted in Virginia, we declared the common law of England to be in force.

The Danger of an All-Powerful Congress

That system of law which has been admired, and has protected us and our ancestors, is excluded by that system. Added to this, we [the state of Virginia] adopted a bill of rights. By this [federal] Constitution, some of the best barriers of human rights are thrown away. Is there not an additional reason to have a bill of rights? By the ancient common law, the trial of all facts is decided by a jury of impartial men from the immediate vicinage. This paper speaks of different juries from the common law in criminal cases; and in civil controversies excludes trial by jury altogether. There is, therefore, more occasion for the supplementary check of a bill of rights now than then. Congress, from their general powers, may fully go into business of human legislation. They may legislate, in criminal cases, from treason to the lowest offence—petty larceny. They may define crimes and prescribe punishments. In the definition of crimes, I trust they will be directed by what wise representatives ought to be governed by. But when we come to punishments, no latitude ought to be left, nor dependence put on the virtue of representatives.

What says [Virginia's] bill of rights?—"that excessive bail ought not to be required, nor excessive fines imposed, nor cruel and unusual punishments inflicted." Are you not, therefore, now calling on those gentlemen who are to compose Congress, to prescribe trials and define punishments without this control? Will they find sentiments there similar to this bill of rights? You let them loose; you do more—you depart from the genius of your country. That paper tells you that the trial of crimes shall be by jury, and held in the state where the crime shall have been committed. Under this extensive provision, they may proceed in a manner extremely dangerous to liberty: a person accused may be carried from one extremity of the state to another, and be tried, not by an impartial jury of the vicinage, acquainted with his character and the circumstances of the fact, but by a jury unacquainted with both, and who may be biased against him. Is not this sufficient to alarm men? How different is this from the immemorial practice of your British ancestors, and your own! I need not tell you that, by the common law, a number of hundredors were required on a jury, and that afterwards it was sufficient if the jurors came from the same county. With less than this the people of England have never been satisfied. That paper ought to have declared the common law in force.

We Must Demand a Bill of Rights for Our Own Safety

In this business of legislation, your members of Congress will loose the restriction of not imposing excessive fines, demanding excessive bail, and inflicting cruel and unusual punishments. These are prohibited by your declaration of rights. What has distinguished our ancestors?—That they would not admit of tortures, or cruel and barbarous punishment. But Congress may introduce the practice of the civil law, in preference to that of the common law. They may introduce the practice of France, Spain, and Germany—of torturing, to extort a confession of the crime. They will say that they might as well draw examples from those countries as from Great Britain, and they will tell you that there is such a necessity of strengthening the arm of government, that they must have a criminal equity, and extort confession by torture, in order to punish with still more relentless severity. We are then lost and undone. And can any man think it troublesome, when we can, by a small interference, prevent our rights from being lost? If you will, like the Virginian government, give them knowledge of the extent of the rights retained by the people, and the powers of themselves, they will, if they be honest men, thank you for it. Will they not wish to go on sure grounds? But if you leave them otherwise, they will not know how to proceed; and, being in a state of uncertainty, they will assume rather than give up powers by implication.

A Bill of Rights Will Settle Disputes

A bill of rights may be summed up in a few words. What do they tell us?—That our rights are reserved. Why not say so? Is it because it will consume too much paper? Gentlemen's reasoning against a bill of rights does not satisfy me. Without saying which has the right side, it remains doubtful. A bill of rights is a favorite thing with the Virginians and the people of the other states likewise. It may be their prejudice, but the government ought to suit their geniuses; otherwise, its operation will be unhappy. A bill of rights, even if its necessity be doubtful, will exclude the possibility of dispute; and, with great submission, I think the best way is to have no dispute.

The Founders Included the Eighth Amendment to Prohibit Torture

Anthony F. Granucci

Anthony F. Granucci traces the history of prohibiting cruel and unusual punishments from biblical times through the framing of the U.S. Constitution. He theorizes that, under English law, the prohibition of outlandish punishments once pertained largely to any punishment that was considered excessive in proportion to the crime. However, Americans interpreted the phrase *cruel and unusual* to apply to the method rather than the degree of punishment. Therefore, the Eighth Amendment was originally a ban against torturous punishments. This article is often referred to by legal scholars and Supreme Court justices who seek a historical framework for the Eighth Amendment. Granucci was a graduate of the University of California at Berkeley and Harvard University before practicing law in California.

The prohibition of excessive punishment, through the establishment of maximum limits, was an early development in the western world. It was first expressed in the Old Testament of the *Bible* in the *Book of Exodus*. One of the laws given to Moses by the God of the Jewish nation, Yahweh, was the *lex talionis*—an eye for an eye, a tooth for a tooth. It is generally considered a law of retribution—the product of a vengeful deity. Envisioning neither mercy nor mitigation of punishment, the *lex talionis* is, by modern standards, extremely harsh; however, it does prescribe a maximum limit

Anthony F. Granucci, "Nor Cruel and Unusual Punishments Inflicted: The Original Meaning," *California Law Review*, vol. 57, October 1969, pp. 844–64. Copyright © 1969 by the *California Law Review*. Reproduced by permission.

on punishment. *Talio* is Latin for "equivalent to" or "equal." That the *lex talionis* requires punishment equal to the crime is made clear by a passage from the *Book of Leviticus:* "If a man injures his neighbor, what he has done must be done to him: broken limb for broken limb, eye for eye, tooth for tooth. As the injury inflicted, so must be the injury suffered."

A Time Line of the Philosophy of Punishment

A concern for equality between the offense and the punishment of the offender was expressed in early Greek philosophy. Aristotle taught that inequality, whether in favor of or against the offender, meant injustice. A similar concept of equality is found in the laws of the Anglos and the Saxons of pre-Norman England. The penal laws of the Germanic peoples in the Middle Ages were enforced through a system of fixed penalties, and the Norse Vikings followed such a system by listing each known crime and its appropriate penalty in the Gulathing and Frustathing Laws. The penalties ranged from outlawry to fines of a few ora. Under the Laws of King Alfred, who reigned in England circa A.D. 900 the *lex talionis* was codified and prescribed in fine detail:

> For a wound in the head if both bones are pierced, 30 shillings shall be given to the injured man,
>
> If the outer bone [only] is pierced, 15 shillings shall be given. . . .
>
> If a wound an inch long is made under the hair, one shilling shall be paid. . . .
>
> If an ear is cut off, 30 shillings shall be paid. . . .
>
> If one knocks out another's eye, he shall pay 66 shillings, 6 1/3 pence. . . .
>
> If the eye is still in the head but the injured man can see nothing with it, one-third of the payment shall be withheld.

The list continues with a monetary value assigned to every part of the anatomy.

Following the Norman conquest of England in 1066, the old system of penalties, which ensured equality between crime and punishment, suddenly disappeared. By the time systematic judicial records were kept, its demise was almost complete. With the exception of certain grave crimes for which the punishment was death or outlawry, the arbitrary fine was replaced by a discretionary amercement. Although amercement's discretionary character allowed the circumstances of each case to be taken into account and the level of cash penalties to be decreased or increased accordingly, the amercement presented an opportunity for excessive or oppressive fines.

The problem of excessive amercements became so prevalent that three chapters of the Magna Carta were devoted to their regulation. [Author F.] Maitland said of Chapter 14 that "very likely there was no clause in the Magna Carta more grateful to the mass of the people." Chapter 14 clearly stipulated as fundamental law a prohibition of excessiveness in punishments:

> A free man shall not be amerced for a trivial offence, except in accordance with the degree of the offence; and for a serious offence he shall be amerced according to its gravity, saving his livelihood; and a merchant likewise, saving his merchandise; in the same way a villein shall be amerced saving his wainage; if they fall into our mercy. And none of the aforesaid amercements shall be imposed except by the testimony of reputable men of the neighborhood.

. . . Thus by the year 1400, we have the expression of "the long standing principle of English law that the punishment should fit the crime. That is, the punishment should not be, by reason of its excessive length or severity, greatly disproportionate to the offense charged" [R. Perry]. In 1615 the King's Bench applied Chapter 14 of the Magna Carta to a "malicious kind of imprisonment" in the case of *Hodges v. Humkin, Mayor of Liskerret:*

> . . . In regard of the manner of this Imprisonment, and of the place where, he being thrown into a Dungeon,

and so to be there kept, without any Bed to lie on, or any bread or meat to eat, and for all these Causes, the Imprisonment was unlawful; Imprisonment ought always to be according to the quality of the offense. . . .

Thus, prior to adoption of the Bill of Rights in 1689 England had developed a common law prohibition against excessive punishments, in any form. Whether the principle was honored in practice or not is an open question. It was reflected in the law reports and charters of England. It is indeed a paradox that the American colonists omitted a prohibition on excessive punishments and adopted instead the prohibition of cruel methods of punishment, which had never existed in English law. . . .

The Role of Robert Beale

By 1689 England had still not developed a prohibition on cruel or barbarous methods of punishment. Although a general policy against excessiveness was expressed repeatedly, objection to particular methods of punishment (except when they were disproportionate to the crime involved) was very rare. The *lex talionis* authorized heinous punishments for heinous crimes. An objection first appears at the end of the sixteenth century, during the early struggles between the Puritans and the established Church of England.

In 1583 the Archbishop of Canterbury, John Whitgift, turned the High Commission into a permanent ecclesiastical court and the Commission began to use torture to extract confessions. Partially because of the use of such inquisitorial methods and partially because of his Puritan beliefs, [law scholar] Sir Robert Beale resigned his place on the Commission. . . .

Late in 1583 Beale published a manuscript entitled *A Book against Oaths Ministered in the Courts of Ecclesiastical Commission*. In it he impugned the right of the crown to fine and imprison persons for ecclesiastical offenses and he condemned the use of torture. Whitgift, defender of the official faith against both catholicism and puritanism, had a "Schedule of Misdemeanors" drawn up against Beale and presented it to the Privy Council. The thirteenth "court" of the schedule was:

He condemneth (without exception of any cause) the racking of grievous offenders as being cruel, barbarous, contrary to law, and unto the liberty of English subjects.

Beale was unique in using Chapter 14 of Magna Carta to argue against the deprivation of ministers. His objections to this deprivation and to cruel punishments in general were also unique in that he even condemned the use of torturous methods when authorized by the royal prerogative. This constituted a significant step beyond other English jurists who, while denying the existence of torture at common law, personally inflicted it upon royal command. Beale thus appears to be the founder of a second principle—that cruel methods of punishment are unlawful. Beale's objections to the use of torture and inquisitorial methods became more and more strident. . . .

Nathaniel Ward's Contribution

A prohibition of cruel methods of punishment was first written into law in America by another Puritan attorney, the Rev. Nathaniel Ward of Ipswich, Masssachusetts. . . .

In early 1634 the [Massachusetts] colony was in a period of political unrest. The Charter of 1629 provided for a government consisting of a governor, a deputy governor, and eighteen assistants (also known as magistrates). The freemen of the colony assembled in a General Court, but the assistants had the power to make laws and inflict punishments. In May 1634, before Ward's arrival, the General Court stripped the assistants of their lawmaking power, and a battle ensued over the assistants' power to veto the General Court's enactments.

One of the major complaints of the freemen was the lack of fundamental laws binding the judicial discretion of the magistrates. Winthrop records in his journal for May 6, 1635:

The deputies having conceived great danger to our state in regard that our magistrates, for want of positive laws, in many cases, might proceed according to their discretions, it was agreed, that some men should be appointed to frame a body of grounds of laws, in resemblance to a Magna Charta, which being allowed by some of the ministers and the general court, should be received for fundamental laws.

The first two committees failed to agree and a third attempt was made in 1638. By [1638] Ward had given up the ministry at Ipswich because of poor health, but being far from incapacitated, he was named to the committee [to draft a framework of laws for Massachusetts]. By 1639 both Rev. Ward and the Rev. John Cotton submitted draft codes to the General Court. The drafts were circulated throughout the colony and in 1641 Ward's draft was enacted into law under the title *Body of Liberties*. Clause 46 of the document read: "For bodily punishments we allow amongst us none that are inhumane, barbarous or cruel." . . .

The Emergence of the Phrase "Cruel and Unusual Punishments"

Fifty years after the drafting of the Massachusetts *Body of Liberties*, and nearly 100 years before the Virginia Declaration of Rights of 1776, the phrase "cruel and unusual punishments" came into being. In the spring of 1688 the shaky reign of King James II was coming to an end. In April he tried and failed to grant a new Declaration of Indulgence to English Catholics. Seven bishops of the Church of England petitioned the King not to publish the declaration and James resolved to have them prosecuted for their insubordinance. Their subsequent acquittal by the King's Bench was an accurate reflection of public sentiment towards the King.

In June the Queen, Mary of Modena, gave birth to a son, an heir to the throne. The birth signaled the coming of the Glorious Revolution. The opposition to James, especially that of William of Orange, could have afforded to await his death and the extinction of the House of Stuart. With a new heir, however, action was needed. On the last day of September, William declared that he would accept the invitation of several English peers to save their nation from "popery." By November 5, 1688, he had crossed the channel with an invasion fleet and risings began in his favor. The King, paralyzed by indecision, let the situation worsen until finally the Queen and baby prince were sent to France for safety. In December James followed, after throwing the great seal of England into the Thames. Lord Chancellor Jeffreys, who had stayed at his post till the end, was captured by rioting mobs and sent to the Tower of London.

The peers of the realm called a parliament to determine the succession to the throne. While debate centered on whether James had abdicated or merely vacated the throne—a point of law crucial to the position of the infant prince—a declaration of rights was drafted which the new monarchs, William and Mary, would ratify. The tenth declaratory clause of the bill reads:

> That excessive bail ought not to be required, nor excessive fines imposed; nor cruel and unusual punishments inflicted.

That clause was transcribed verbatim into the Virginia Declaration of Rights of 1776 and, with the substitution of "shall" for "ought," now appears in the eighth amendment to the United States Constitution.

The "Bloody Assize"

Noting the obvious linguistic link between the Virginia Declaration of Rights and the English Bill of Rights, legal historians have searched for the types of punishments which the drafters of the latter document sought to prohibit. Most historians point to the treason trials of 1685—the "Bloody Assize" —which followed the abortive rebellion of the Duke of Monmouth and the opinion that the cruel and unusual punishments clause was directed to the conduct of Chief Justice Jeffreys during these trials is still in vogue. After Charles II died in February 1685, his brother succeeded him as James II. Charles' eldest illegitimate son, the new King's nephew, James, Duke of Monmouth was in exile in Holland at the time. Monmouth, a fervent Anglican, had been associated with the Whigs of the Country Party. An invasion was planned and executed from Holland, where Monmouth was allowed the use of Dutch ports by William, Prince of Orange.

A small force led by Monmouth landed in western England on June 11, 1685. He proclaimed himself King, but his army was quickly defeated at the Battle of Sedgemoor. Within a month Monmouth was taken prisoner and was executed in London. The abortive rebellion had caused the cancellation of the autumn assize of 1685 and the King appointed Chief Justice Jeffreys of the King's Bench to head a special commission to travel the western circuit and try the captured rebels.

The assize began in late August with the trial of Alice Lisle, a 71 year-old widow, for the crime harboring rebels. John Lisle, her late husband, had been the President of Cromwell's High Court of Justice and had participated in the events leading to the execution of Charles I. Lisle had been excepted from the restoration and had been murdered abroad by royalist agents in 1664. Mrs. Lisle was convicted and sentenced to be burned alive, the traditional penalty for woman felons. The King commuted her sentence to beheading. When the Jeffreys commission reached Dorchester, it became apparent that to try each rebel separately would require an inordinate amount of time. At this point, Sir Henry Pollfexen, a Whig attorney who had been appointed chief prosecutor for the special commission, and the Chief Justice engaged in mass plea-bargaining. Pollfexen let it be known that no one who pleaded guilty would suffer the death penalty. The penalty for treason at that time consisted of drawing the condemned man on a cart to the gallows, where he was hanged by the neck, cut down while still alive, disembowelled and his bowels burnt before him, and then beheaded and quartered. Word of Pollfexen's proposal spread and in a matter of days over 500 trials were completed. Those who had pleaded not guilty but were found guilty were immediately executed. No one who pleaded guilty was executed during the period of the commission itself. However the bargain was not fully kept. Almost 200 prisioners who had pleaded guilty were executed during the winter. Jeffreys signed the death warrants himself before his return to London, where James II rewarded him with the Lord Chancellorship.

The assize was widely publicized by Puritan pamphleteers after 1689. One influential version was by Titus Oates . . . and was titled *The Western Martyrology or, The Bloody Assize*. The persuasive effect of the Puritan propaganda made Jeffreys the scapegoat for the abuses of the Stuart period and influenced later historians like G.M. Trevelyan to write: "The revenge taken upon the rebels . . . by . . . Judge Jeffreys in his insane lust for cruelty, was stimulated by orders from the King." Propaganda prevailed, and history has recorded that the cruel and unusual punishments clause was in answer to the "Bloody Assize." A close examination of the legislative history of the Bill of Rights produces a quite different conclusion. . . .

Unauthorized and Disproportionate

The original draft of [the English Bill of Rights, dated] February 2 [1689] speaks of illegal punishments. The document of February 12 complains of "illegal and cruel punishments" and then continues to prohibit "cruel and unusual punishments." No contemporary document gives any reason for the change in language. Indeed, John Somers, reputed draftsman of the Bill of Rights, wrote later of the "horrible and illegal" punishments used during the Stuart regime. The final phraseology, especially the use of the word "unusual," must be laid simply to chance and sloppy draftsmanship. There is no evidence to connect the cruel and unusual punishments clause with the "Bloody Assize." On the contrary, everything points away from any connection. . . .

In the seventeenth century, the word "cruel" had a less onerous meaning than it has today. In normal usage it simply meant severe or hard. The *Oxford English Dictionary* quotes as representative Jonathan Swift, who wrote in 1710, "I have got a cruel cold, and staid within all this day." Sir William Blackstone, discussing the problem of "punishments of unreasonable severity," uses the word "cruel" as a synonym for severe or excessive.

The English evidence shows that the cruel and unusual punishments clause of the Bill of Rights of 1689 was first, an objection to the imposition of punishments which were unauthorized by statute and outside the jurisdiction of the sentencing court, and second, a reiteration of the English policy against disproportionate penalties. Nevertheless, it is clear that the American framers read into the phrase the meaning of Beale and Ward. How, then, did the American framers obtain their interpretation of the cruel and unusual punishments clause, an interpretation opposite to that of the English view?

The American Misinterpretation

George Mason and the framers of the American Constitution misinterpreted the meaning of the cruel and unusual punishments clause of the English Bill of Rights of 1689. . . . The shift in meaning was apparently not deliberate; either Mason copied the clause without any understanding as to its original meaning, arbitrarily intending his own interpretation drawn from colonial sources, or he and his contemporaries had a distorted notion of its meaning derived from the English legal treatises available at the time. . . .

The only treatise which discussed the topic of punishment was the fourth volume of [Sir William] Blackstone's *Commentaries [on the Laws of England,* 1768]. Volume four was published in London in 1768 and sent to the colonies soon thereafter. Demand for Blackstone's work was heavy in the colonies and his influence on the formation of American law was great. In 1775 Edmund Burke is reported to have told the House of Commons that almost as many copies of the *Commentaries* had been sold in America as in the whole of England.

Chapter 29 of volume four is entitled "Judgment and Its Consequences." The chapter begins with a description of the methods available to arrest a judgment in a criminal case. The next three pages . . . contain the germ of a misinterpretation which still infects our view of the eighth amendment.

> If all these resources fail, the court must pronounce that judgment which the law has annexed to the crime, and which has been constantly mentioned, together with the crime itself, in some or other of the former chapters. Of these some are capital, which extend to the life of the offender, and consist generally in being hanged by the neck till dead; though in very atrocious crimes other circumstances of terror, pain or disgrace are super-added: as, in treasons of all kinds, being drawn or dragged to

the place of execution; in high treason affecting the king's person or government, embowelling alive, beheading and quartering; and in murder, a public dissection. And, in case of any treason committed by a female, the judgment is to be burned alive. But the humanity of the English nation has authorized, by a tacit consent, an almost general mitigation of such part of these judgments as savor of torture or cruelty: A sledge or hurdle being usually allowed to such traitors as are condemned to be drawn; and there being very few instances (and those accidental or by negligence) of any person's being embowelled or burned, till previously deprived of sensation by strangling. Some punishments consist in exile or banishment, by abjuration of the realm, or transportation to the American colonies: others in loss of liberty, by perpetual or temporary imprisonment. Some extend to confiscation, by forfeiture of lands, or moveables, or both, or of the profits of lands for life: others induce a disability, of holding offices or employments, being heirs, executors, and the like. Some, though rarely, occasion a mutilation or dismembering, by cutting off the hand or ears: others fix a lasting stigma on the offender, by slitting the nostrils, or branding in the hand or face. Some are merely pecuniary, by stated or discretionary fines, and lastly there are others, that consist primarily in their ignominity, though most of them are mixed with some degree of corporal pain; and these are inflicted chiefly for crimes, which arise from indigence, or which render even opulence disgraceful. Such as whipping, hard labor in the house of correction, the pillory, the stocks, and the duckingstool. . . .

It should be noted that Blackstone's England draws, beheads, burns, and quarters, slits noses and mutilates felons. Those other punishments that "savor of torture or cruelty" are prohibited, not by statute, but by the "tacit consent" of the English people. There is no citation to the Bill of Rights of 1689 for such a prohibition. Blackstone continues with a discussion of discretionary punishment, especially the fine. . . .

In his discussion of fines Blackstone finds it necessary to cite the Bill of Rights—a citation he had not found necessary when discussing torture—to show that fines are regulated by law. He completes his quote of the excessive fines clause with the cruel and unusual punishments clause. . . .

But Blackstone can be misread as citing the cruel and unusual punishments clause for a prohibition of the tortures. . . . The passages . . . were so read by the Supreme Court of Delaware in a [1963] case upholding the use of lashes as a punishment in that state. . . .

If such an unjustified reading of Blackstone can be made in 1963 by the Supreme Court of Delaware, a similar reading could have been made by George Mason and others at the Virginia Convention of 1776. It is submitted that such a reading explains the American framer's interpretation of the cruel and unusual punishments clause; an interpretation which spawned the American doctrine that the words "cruel and unusual" proscribed not excessive but torturous punishments.

The Supreme Court Expands the Definition of Cruel and Unusual Punishment

Joseph McKenna

In 1910 the U.S. Supreme Court ruled on *Weems v. United States*, which questioned the severity of punishment prescribed to Paul Weems. Weems was a disbursing officer with the U.S. Coast Guard stationed in the Philippine Islands. He was convicted of falsifying records, thereby defrauding the government of 612 pesos. His sentence, known as *cadena temporal* under the Philippine Code, included fifteen years in prison with hard labor, the constant use of chains to constrain him, the loss of all political rights during imprisonment, and a fine. He also became subject to permanent surveillance after his release. Weems appealed his conviction on the grounds that its severity constituted cruel and unusual punishment; the U.S. Supreme Court agreed in a four-to-two decision. *Weems* is considered a benchmark case because it broadened the definition of *cruel and unusual* to include more than just torturous physical punishment. More than 120 years after the Bill of Rights was ratified, the Supreme Court shifted its interpretation of the Eighth Amendment from what was considered cruel and unusual by the framers of the Constitution in 1789 (a historical interpretation that included restricting punishments such as whippings and the lopping off of one's ear) to what was considered cruel and unusual according to society's evolving standards. This ruling thus marks the beginning of the Court's interpreting the Eighth Amendment as having an "expansive and vital character," or one with an evolving nature

Joseph McKenna, majority opinion, *Weems v. United States,* 217 U.S. 349, 1910.

that takes into account current punishment standards. Joseph McKenna served on the Supreme Court from 1898 to 1925.

What constitutes a cruel and unusual punishment has not been exactly decided. It has been said that ordinarily the terms imply something inhuman and barbarous,— torture and the like [*McDonald v. Commonwealth of Massachusetts,* 1901]. The court, however, in that case, conceded the possibility 'that punishment in the state prison for a long term of years might be so disproportionate to the offense as to constitute a cruel and unusual punishment.' Other cases have selected certain tyrannical acts of the English monarchs as illustrating the meaning of the clause and the extent of its prohibition.

The 'Indefinite' Nature of 'Cruel and Unusual'

The provision received very little debate in Congress. We find from the Congressional Register, p. 225, that Mr. Smith, of South Carolina, 'objected to the words "nor cruel and unusual punishment," the import of them being too indefinite.' Mr. Livermore opposed the adoption of the clause saying:

> The clause seems to express a great deal of humanity, on which account I have no objection to it; but, as it seems to have no meaning in it, I do not think it necessary. What is meant by the terms 'excessive bail?' Who are to be the judges? What is understood by 'excessive fines?' It lays with the court to determine. No cruel and unusual punishment is to be inflicted; it is sometimes necessary to hang a man, villains often deserve whipping, and perhaps having their ears cut off; but are we, in future, to be prevented from inflicting these punishments because they are cruel? If a more lenient mode of correcting vice and deterring others from the commission of it could be invented, it would be very prudent in the legislature to adopt it; but until we have some security that this will be done, we ought not to be restrained from making necessary laws by any declaration of this kind.

The question was put on the clause, and it was agreed to by a considerable majority.

The Supreme Court Has Yet to Define 'Cruel and Unusual'

No case has occurred in this court which has called for an exhaustive definition. In *Pervear v. Massachusetts* [1866], it was decided that the clause did not apply to state but to national legislation. But we went further, and said that we perceive nothing excessive, or cruel, or unusual in a fine of $50 and imprisonment at hard labor in the house of correction for three months, which was imposed for keeping and maintaining, without a license, a tenement for the illegal sale and illegal keeping of intoxicating liquors. A decision from which no one will dissent.

In *Wilkerson v. Utah* [1879], the clause came up again for consideration. A statute of Utah provided that 'a person convicted of a capital offense should suffer death by being shot, hanged, or beheaded,' as the court might direct, or he should 'have his option as to the manner of his execution.' The statute was sustained. The court pointed out that death was an usual punishment for murder, that it prevailed in the territory for many years, and was inflicted by shooting; also that that mode of execution was usual under military law. It was hence concluded that it was not forbidden by the Constitution of the United States as cruel or unusual. The court quoted [English lawyer William] Blackstone as saying that the sentence of death was generally executed by hanging, but also that circumstances of terror, pain, or disgrace were sometimes superadded. 'Cases mentioned by the author,' the court said, 'are where the person was drawn or dragged to the place of execution, in treason; or where he was disemboweled alive, beheaded, and quartered, in high treason. Mention is also made of public dissection in murder and burning alive in treason committed by a female.' . . .

This court's final commentary was that 'difficulty would attend the effort to define with exactness the extent of the constitutional provision which provides that cruel and unusual punishments shall not be inflicted; but it is safe to affirm that punishments of torture, such as those mentioned by the commentator referred to, and all others in the same line of unnecessary cruelty, are forbidden by that Amendment to the Constitution' [Thomas McIntyre Cooley, 1868].

That passage was quoted *in Re Kemmler* [1890] and this comment was made: 'Punishments are cruel when they involve torture or a lingering death; but the punishment of death is not cruel, within the meaning of that word as used in the Constitution. It implies there something inhuman and barbarous, and something more than the mere extinguishment of life.' The case was an application for habeas corpus, and went off on a question of jurisdiction, this court holding that the 8th Amendment did not apply to state legislation. It was not meant in the language we have quoted to give a comprehensive definition of cruel and unusual punishment, but only to explain the application of the provision to the punishment of death. In other words, to describe what might make the punishment of death cruel and unusual, though of itself it is not so. It was found as a fact by the state court that death by electricity was more humane than death by hanging.

In *O'Neil v. Vermont* [1892] the question was raised, but not decided. The reasons given for this were that because it was not as a Federal question assigned as error, and, so far as it arose under the Constitution of Vermont, it was not within the province of the court to decide. Moreover, it was said, as a Federal question, it had always been ruled that the 8th Amendment of the Constitution of the United States did not apply to the states. Mr. Justice Field, Mr. Justice Harlan, and Mr. Justice Brewer were of opinion that the question was presented, and Mr. Justice Field, construing the clause of the Constitution prohibiting the infliction of cruel and unusual punishment, said, the other two justices concurring, that the inhibition was directed not only against punishments which inflict torture, 'but against all punishments which, by their excessive length or severity, are greatly disproportioned to the offenses charged.' He said further: 'The whole inhibition is against that which is excessive in the bail required or fine imposed or punishment inflicted.'

The Motive of the Clause

The law writers are indefinite. [Supreme Court justice Joseph] Story, in his work on the Constitution, says that the provision 'is an exact transcript of a clause in the Bill of Rights framed at the [British] revolution of 1688.' He expressed the view that the provision 'would seem to be wholly unnecessary in a free government, since it is scarcely possible that any department of such a government should authorize or justify such atrocious conduct.' He, however, observed that it was 'adopted as an admonition to all departments of the national department, to warn them against such violent proceedings as had taken place in England in the arbitrary reigns of some of the Stuarts' [a British royal family]. . . . If the learned author meant by this to confine the prohibition of the provision to such penalties and punishment as were inflicted by the Stuarts, his citations do not sustain him. . . . The . . . citations are of the remarks of Patrick Henry in the Virginia convention, and of Mr. Wilson in the Pennsylvania convention. Patrick Henry said that there was danger in the adoption of the Constitution without a Bill of Rights. Mr. Wilson considered that it was unnecessary, and had been purposely omitted from the Constitution. Both, indeed, referred to the tyranny of the Stuarts. Henry said that the people of England, in the Bill of Rights, prescribed to William, Prince of Orange, upon what terms he should reign. Wilson said that 'the doctrine and practice of a declaration of rights have been borrowed from the conduct of the people of England on some remarkable occasions; but the principles and maxims on which their government is constituted are widely different from those of ours.' It appears, therefore, that Wilson, and those who thought like Wilson, felt sure that the spirit of liberty could be trusted, and that its ideals would be represented, not debased, by legislation. Henry and those who believed as he did would take no chances. Their predominant political impulse was distrust of power, and they insisted on constitutional limitations against its abuse. But surely they intended more than to register a fear of the forms of abuse that went out of practice with the Stuarts. Surely, their jealousy of power had a saner justification than that. They were men of action, practical and sagacious, not beset with vain imagining, and it must have come to them that there could be exercises of cruelty by laws other than those which inflicted bodily pain or mutilation. With power in a legislature great, if not unlimited, to give criminal character to the actions of men, with power unlimited to fix terms of imprisonment with what accompaniments they might, what more potent instrument of cruelty could be put into the hands of power? And it was believed that power might be tempted to cruelty. This was the motive of the clause, and if we are to attribute an intelligent providence to its advocates we cannot think that it was intended to prohibit only practices like the Stuarts', or to prevent only an exact repetition of history. We cannot think that the possibility of a coercive cruelty being exercised through other forms of punishment was overlooked. We say 'coercive cruelty,' because there was more to be considered than the ordinary criminal laws. Cruelty might become an instrument of tyranny; of zeal for a purpose, either honest or sinister.

Vital Principles Have Wide, Dynamic Applications

Legislation, both statutory and constitutional, is enacted, it is true, from an experience of evils but its general language should not, therefore, be necessarily confined to the form that evil had theretofore taken. Time works changes, brings into existence new conditions and purposes. Therefore a principle, to be vital, must be capable of wider application than the mischief which gave it birth. This is peculiarly true of constitutions. They are not ephemeral enactments, designed to meet passing occasions. They are, to use the words of Chief Justice Marshall, 'designed to approach immortality as nearly as human institutions can approach it.' The future is their care, and provision for events of good and bad tendencies of which no prophecy can be made. In the application of a constitution, therefore, our contemplation cannot be only of what has been, but of what may be. Under any other rule a constitution would indeed be as easy of application as it would be deficient in efficacy and power. Its general principles would have little value, and be converted by precedent into impotent and lifeless formulas. Rights declared in words might be lost in reality. And this has been recognized. The meaning and vitality of the Constitution have developed against narrow and restrictive construction. . . .

The Sentence of *Cadena Temporal* Is Excessive and Cruel

We turn back to the law in controversy. Its character and the cointence in this case may be illustrated by examples even better than it can be represented by words. There are degrees of homicide that are not punished so severely, nor are the following crimes: misprision of treason, inciting rebellion, conspiracy to destroy the government by force, recruiting soldiers in the United States to fight against the United States, forgery of letters patent, forgery of bonds and other instruments for the purpose of defrauding the United States, robbery, larceny, and other crimes. Section 86 of the Penal Laws of the United States, as revised and amended by the act of Congress of March 4, 1909, provides that any person charged with the payment of any appropriation made by Congress, who shall pay to any clerk or other employee of the United States a sum less than that provided by law, and require a receipt for a sum greater than that paid to and received by him, shall be guilty of embezzlement, and shall be fined in double the amount so withheld, and imprisoned not more than two years. The offense described has similarity to the offense for which Weems was convicted, but the punishment provided for it is in great contrast to the penalties of *cadena temporal* and its 'accessories.' If we turn to the legislation of the Philippine Commission we find that instead of the penalties of *cadena temporal*, medium degree (fourteen years, eight months, and one day, to seventeen years and four months, with fine 'accessories'), to *cadena perpetua*, fixed by the Spanish Penal Code for the falsification of bank notes and other instruments authorized by the law of the kingdom, it is provided that the forgery of or counterfeiting the obligations or securities of the United States or of the Philippine Islands shall be punished by a fine of not more than 10,000 pesos and by imprisonment of not more than fifteen years. In other words, the highest punishment possible for a crime which may cause the loss of many thousands of dollars, and to prevent which the duty of the state should be as eager as to prevent the perversion of truth in a public document, is not greater than that which may be imposed for falsifying a single item of a public account. And this contrast shows more than different exercises of legislative judgment. It is greater than that. It condemns the sentence in this case as cruel and unusual. It exhibits a difference between unrestrained power and that which is exercised under the spirit of constitutional limitations formed to establish justice. The state thereby suffers nothing and loses no power. The purpose of punishment is fulfilled, crime is repressed by penalties of just, not tormenting, severity, its repetition is prevented, and hope is given for the reformation of the criminal. . . .

It follows from these views that, even if the minimum penalty of *cadena temporal* had been imposed, it would have been repugnant to the Bill of Rights. In other words, the fault is in the law; and, as we are pointed to no other under which a sentence can be imposed, the judgment must be reversed, with directions to dismiss the proceedings.

So ordered.

CHAPTER TWO

The Eighth Amendment and the Death Penalty

The Bill of Rights

The Death Penalty Is Declared Unconstitutional

William J. Brennan Jr.

William Henry Furman, a black man, had been convicted in the state of Georgia for burglarizing a home and, in attempting to flee, accidentally shooting and killing a resident. In *Furman v. Georgia* (1972) Furman appealed his death sentence on the grounds that the jury had received no guidelines or instructions on what constitutes a "heinous" crime (which in Georgia warranted the use of the death penalty). His sentence, he argued, was therefore unconstitutional in that it was cruel and unusual. In this landmark Supreme Court case, the Court went a step further: Capital punishment as a whole was judged unconstitutional. It was deemed cruel and unusual based on four determining principles. The first principle was that a punishment must not be so severe as to be degrading to human beings. The second principle was that the state must not arbitrarily inflict an unusually severe punishment. Principle three was that a severe punishment must not be unacceptable to contemporary society. The fourth and final principle was that severe punishment must not be excessive. According to the Court, the death penalty violated all four principles, with particular disregard for the second principle since there were apparent discrepancies in its administration with regard to race and other factors. William J. Brennan Jr. served on the Supreme Court from 1956 to 1990.

The question . . . is whether the deliberate infliction of death is today consistent with the command of the Clause that the State may not inflict punishments that do not com-

William J. Brennan Jr., majority opinion, *Furman v. Georgia,* 408 U.S. 238, 1972.

port with human dignity. I will analyze the punishment of death in terms of the [four] principles [for determining whether a punishment comports with human dignity] and the cumulative test to which they lead: It is a denial of human dignity, for the State arbitrarily to subject a person to an unusually severe punishment that society has indicated it does not regard as acceptable, and that cannot be shown to serve any penal purpose more effectively than a significantly less drastic punishment. Under these principles and this test, death is today a 'cruel and unusual' punishment.

On Principle One: Death Is a Uniquely Severe Punishment

Death is a unique punishment in the United States. In a society that so strongly affirms the sanctity of life, not surprisingly the common view is that death is the ultimate sanction. This natural human feeling appears all about us. There has been no national debate about punishment, in general or by imprisonment, comparable to the debate about the punishment of death. No other punishment has been so continuously restricted, nor has any State yet abolished prisons, as some have abolished this punishment. And those States that still inflict death reserve it for the most heinous crimes. Juries, of course, have always treated death cases differently, as have governors exercising their commutation powers. Criminal defendants are of the same view. 'As all practicing lawyers know, who have defended persons charged with capital offenses, often the only goal possible is to avoid the death penalty' *Griffin v. Illinois* [1956]. Some legislatures have required particular procedures, such as two-stage trials and automatic appeals, applicable only in death cases. 'It is the universal experience in the administration of criminal justice that those charged with capital offenses are granted special considerations' [*Griffin*]. . . . This Court, too, almost always treats death cases as a class apart. And the unfortunate effect of this punishment upon the functioning of the judicial process is well known; no other punishment has a similar effect.

The only explanation for the uniqueness of death is its extreme severity. Death is today an unusually severe punishment, unusual in its pain, in its finality, and in its enormity. No other existing punishment is comparable to death in terms of physical and mental suffering. Although our information is not conclusive, it appears that there is no method available that guarantees an immediate and painless death. Since the discontinuance of flogging as a constitutionally permissible punishment, death remains as the only punishment that may involve the conscious infliction of physical pain. In addition, we know that mental pain is an inseparable part of our practice of punishing criminals by death, for the prospect of pending execution exacts a frightful toll during the inevitable long wait between the imposition of sentence and the actual infliction of death. . . .

The unusual severity of death is manifested most clearly in its finality and enormity. Death, in these respects, is in a class by itself. . . .

Death is truly an awesome punishment. The calculated killing of a human being by the State involves, by its very nature, a denial of the executed person's humanity. The contrast with the plight of a person punished by imprisonment is evident. An individual in prison does not lose 'the right to have rights.' A prisoner retains, for example, the constitutional rights to the free exercise of religion, to be free of cruel and unusual punishments, and to treatment as a 'person' for purposes of due process of law and the equal protection of the laws. A prisoner remains a member of the human family. Moreover, he retains the right of access to the courts. His punishment is not irrevocable. Apart from the common charge, grounded upon the recognition of human fallibility, that the punishment of death must inevitably be inflicted upon innocent men, we know that death has been the lot of men whose convictions were unconstitutionally secured in view of later, retroactively applied, holdings of this Court. The punishment itself may have been unconstitutionally inflicted, yet the finality of death precludes relief. . . .

On Principle Two: The Death Sentence Is Arbitrarily Inflicted

In comparison to all other punishments today, then, the deliberate extinguishment of human life by the State is uniquely degrading to human dignity. I would not hesitate to hold, on that ground alone, that death is today a 'cruel and unusual' punishment, were it not that death is a punishment of long-standing usage and acceptance in this country. I therefore turn to the second principle—that the State may not arbitrarily inflict an unusually severe punishment.

The outstanding characteristic of our present practice of punishing criminals by death is the infrequency with which we resort to it. The evidence is conclusive that death is not the ordinary punishment for any crime.

There has been a steady decline in the infliction of this punishment in every decade since the 1930's, the earliest period for which accurate statistics are available. In the 1930's, executions averaged 167 per year; in the 1940's, the average was 128; in the 1950's, it was 72; and in the years 1960–1962, it was 48. There have been a total of 46 executions since then, 36 of them in 1963–1964. Yet our population and the number of capital crimes committed have increased greatly over the past four decades. The contemporary rarity of the infliction of this punishment is thus the end result of a long-continued decline. That rarity is plainly revealed by an examination of the years 1961–1970, the last 10-year period for which statistics are available. During that time, an average of 106 death sentences was imposed each year. Not nearly that number, however, could be carried out, for many were precluded by commutations to life or a term of years, transfers to mental institutions because of insanity, resentences to life or a term of years, grants of new trials and orders for resentencing, dismissals of indictments and reversals of convictions, and deaths by suicide and natural causes. On January 1, 1961, the death row population was 219; on December 31, 1970, it was 608; during that span, there were 135 executions. Consequently, had the 389 additions to death row also been executed the annual average would have been 52. In short, the country might, at most, have executed one criminal each week. In fact, of course, far fewer were executed. Even before the moratorium on executions began in 1967, executions totaled only 42 in 1961 and 47 in 1962, an average of less than one per week; the number dwindled to 21 in 1963, to 15 in 1964, and to seven in 1965; in 1966, there was one execution, and in 1967, there were two.

When a country of over 200 million people inflicts an unusually severe punishment no more than 50 times a year, the inference is strong that the punishment is not being regularly and fairly applied.

To dispel it would indeed require a clear showing of nonarbitrary infliction.

Although there are no exact figures available, we know that thousands of murders and rapes are committed annually in States where death is an authorized punishment for those crimes. However the rate of infliction is characterized —as 'freakishly' or 'spectacularly' rare, or simply as rare—it would take the purest sophistry to deny that death is inflicted in only a minute fraction of these cases. How much rarer, after all, could the infliction of death be?

When the punishment of death is inflicted in a trivial number of the cases in which it is legally available, the conclusion is virtually inescapable that it is being inflicted arbitrarily. Indeed, it smacks of little more than a lottery system. The States claim, however, that this rarity is evidence not of arbitrariness, but of informed selectivity: Death is inflicted, they say, only in 'extreme' cases.

Informed selectivity, of course, is a value not to be denigrated. Yet presumably the States could make precisely the same claim if there were 10 executions per year, or five, or even if there were but one. That there may be as many as 50 per year does not strengthen the claim. When the rate of infliction is at this low level, it is highly implausible that only the worst criminals or the criminals who commit the worst crimes are selected for this punishment. No one has yet suggested a rational basis that could differentiate in those terms the few who die from the many who go to prison. Crimes and criminals simply do not admit of a distinction that can be drawn so finely as to explain, on that ground, the execution of such a tiny sample of those eligible. Certainly the laws that provide for this punishment do not attempt to draw that distinction; all cases to which the laws apply are necessarily 'extreme.' Nor is the distinction credible in fact. If, for example, petitioner [William Henry] Furman or his crime illustrates the 'extreme,' then nearly all murderers and their murders are also 'extreme.' Furthermore, our procedures in death cases, rather than resulting in the selection of 'extreme' cases for this punishment, actually sanction an arbitrary selection. For this Court has held that juries may, as they do, make the decision whether to impose a death sentence wholly unguided by standards governing that decision. In other words, our procedures are not constructed to guard against the totally capricious selection of criminals for the punishment of death.

Although it is difficult to imagine what further facts would be necessary in order to prove that death is, as my Brother [fellow Supreme Court justice Potter]Stewart puts it, 'wantonly and . . . freakishly' inflicted, I need not conclude that arbitrary infliction is patently obvious. I am not considering this punishment by the isolated light of one principle. The probability of arbitrariness is sufficiently substantial that it can be relied upon, in combination with the other principles, in reaching a judgment on the constitutionality of this punishment.

On Principle Three: Death Is Unacceptable to Contemporary Society

When there is a strong probability that an unusually severe and degrading punishment is being inflicted arbitrarily, we may well expect that society will disapprove of its infliction. I turn, therefore, to the third principle. An examination of the history and present operation of the American practice of punishing criminals by death reveals that this punishment has been almost totally rejected by contemporary society.

I cannot add to my Brother [Supreme Court justice Thurgood] Marshall's comprehensive treatment of the English and American history of this punishment. I emphasize, however, one significant conclusion that emerges from that history. From the beginning of our Nation, the punishment of death has stirred acute public controversy. Although pragmatic arguments for and against the punishment have been frequently advanced, this longstanding and heated controversy cannot be explained solely as the result of differences over the practical wisdom of a particular government policy. At bottom, the battle has been waged on moral grounds. The country has debated whether a society for which the dignity of the individual is the supreme value can, without a fundamental inconsistency, follow the practice of deliberately putting some of its members to death. . . . It is this essentially moral conflict that forms the backdrop for the past changes in and the present operation of our system of imposing death as a punishment for crime.

Our practice of punishing criminals by death has changed greatly over the years. One significant change has been in our methods of inflicting death. Although this country never embraced the more violent and repulsive methods employed in England, we did for a long time rely almost exclusively upon the gallows and the firing squad. Since the development of the supposedly more humane methods of electrocution late in the 19th century and lethal gas in the 20th, however, hanging and shooting have virtually ceased. Our concern for decency and human dignity, moreover, has compelled changes in the circumstances surrounding the execution itself. No longer does our society countenance the spectacle of public executions, once thought desirable as a deterrent to criminal behavior by others. Today we reject public executions as debasing and brutalizing to us all.

Also significant is the drastic decrease in the crimes for which the punishment of death is actually inflicted. While esoteric capital crimes remain on the books, since 1930 murder and rape have accounted for nearly 99% of the total executions, and murder alone for about 87%. . . .

Virtually all death sentences today are discretionarily imposed. Finally, it is significant that nine States no longer inflict the punishment of death under any circumstances, and five others have restricted it to extremely rare crimes.

Thus, although 'the death penalty has been employed throughout our history' [*Trop v. Dulles*, 1958], in fact the history of this punishment is one of successive restriction. What was once a common punishment has become, in the context of a continuing moral debate, increasingly rare. The evolution of this punishment evidences, not that it is an inevitable part of the American scene, but that it has proved progressively more troublesome to the national conscience. The result of this movement is our current system of administering the punishment, under which death sentences are rarely imposed and death is even more rarely inflicted. It is, of course, 'We, the People' who are responsible for the rarity both of the imposition and the carrying out of this punishment. Juries, 'express(ing) the conscience of the community on the ultimate question of life or death' [*Witherspoon v. Illinois*, 1968] have been able to bring themselves to vote for death in a mere 100 or so cases among the thousands tried each year where the punishment is available. Governors, elected by and acting for us, have regularly commuted a substantial number of those sentences. And it is our society that insists upon due process of law to the end that no person will be unjustly put to death, thus ensuring that many more of those sentences will not be carried out. In sum, we have made death a rare punishment today.

The progressive decline in, and the current rarity of, the infliction of death demonstrate that our society seriously questions the appropriateness of this punishment today. The States point out that many legislatures authorize death as the punishment for certain crimes and that substantial segments of the public, as reflected in opinion polls and referendum votes, continue to support it. Yet the availability of this punishment through statutory authorization, as well as the polls and referenda, which amount simply to approval of that authorization, simply underscores the extent to which our society has in fact rejected this punishment. When an unusually severe punishment is authorized for wide-scale application but not, because of society's refusal, inflicted save in a few instances, the inference is compelling that there is a deep-seated reluctance to inflict it. Indeed, the likelihood is great that the punishment is tolerated only because of its disuse. The objective indicator of society's view of an unusually severe punishment is what society does with it, and today society will inflict death upon only a small sample of the eligible criminals. Rejection could hardly be more complete without becoming absolute. At the very least, I must conclude that contemporary society views this punishment with substantial doubt.

On Principle Four: Death Is Excessive

The final principle to be considered is that an unusually severe and degrading punishment may not be excessive in view of the purposes for which it is inflicted. This principle, too, is related to the others. When there is a strong probability that the State is arbitrarily inflicting an unusually severe punishment that is subject to grave societal doubts, it is likely also that the punishment cannot be shown to be serving any penal purpose that could not be served equally well by some less severe punishment.

The States' primary claim is that death is a necessary punishment because it prevents the commission of capital crimes more effectively than any less severe punishment. The first part of this claim is that the infliction of death is necessary to stop the individuals executed from committing further crimes. The sufficient answer to this is that if a criminal convicted of a capital crime poses a danger to society, effective administration of the State's pardon and parole laws can delay or deny his release from prison, and techniques of isolation can eliminate or minimize the danger while he remains confined.

The more significant argument is that the threat of death prevents the commission of capital crimes because it deters potential criminals who would not be deterred by the threat of imprisonment. The argument is not based upon evidence that the threat of death is a superior deterrent. Indeed, as my Brother Marshall establishes, the available evidence uniformly indicates, although it does not conclusively prove, that the threat of death has no greater deterrent effect than the threat of imprisonment. The States argue, however, that they are entitled to rely upon common human experience, and that experience, they say, supports the conclusion that death must be a more effective deterrent than any less severe punishment. Because people fear death the most, the argument runs, the threat of death must be the greatest deterrent.

It is important to focus upon the precise import of this argument. It is not denied that many, and probably most, capital crimes cannot be deterred by the threat of punishment. Thus the argument can apply only to those who think rationally about the commission of capital crimes. Particularly is that true when the potential criminal, under this argument, must not only consider the risk of punishment, but also distinguish between two possible punishments. The concern, then, is with a particular type of potential criminal, the rational person who will commit a capital crime knowing that the punishment is long-term imprisonment, which may well be for the rest of his life, but will not commit the crime knowing that the punishment is death. On the face of it, the assumption that such persons exist is implausible.

In any event, this argument cannot be appraised in the abstract. We are not presented with the theoretical question whether under any imaginable circumstances the threat of death might be a greater deterrent to the commission of capital crimes than the threat of imprisonment. We are concerned with the practice of punishing criminals by death as it exists in the United States today. Proponents of this argument necessarily admit that its validity depends upon the existence of a system in which the punishment of death is invariably and swiftly imposed. Our system, of course, satisfies neither condition. A rational person contemplating a murder or rape is confronted, not with the certainty of a speedy death, but with the slightest possibility that he will be executed in the distant future. The risk of death is remote and improbable; in contrast, the risk of long-term imprisonment is near and great. In short, whatever the speculative validity of the assumption that the threat of death is a superior deterrent, there is no reason to believe that as currently administered the punishment of death is necessary to deter the commission of capital crimes. Whatever might be the case were all or substantially all eligible criminals quickly put to death, unverifiable possibilities are an insufficient basis upon which to conclude that the threat of death today has any greater deterrent efficacy than the threat of imprisonment.

There is, however, another aspect to the argument that the punishment of death is necessary for the protection of society. The infliction of death, the States urge, serves to manifest the community's outrage at the commission of the crime. It is, they say, a concrete public expression of moral indignation that inculcates respect for the law and helps assure a more peaceful community. Moreover, we are told, not only does the punishment of death exert this widespread moralizing influence upon community values, it also satisfies the popular demand for grievous condemnation of abhorrent crimes and thus prevents disorder, lynching, and attempts by private citizens to take the law into their own hands.

The question, however, is not whether death serves these supposed purposes of punishment, but whether death serves them more effectively than imprisonment. There is no evidence whatever that utilization of imprisonment rather than death encourages private blood feuds and other disorders. Surely if there were such a danger, the execution of a handful of criminals each year would not prevent it. The assertion that death alone is a sufficiently emphatic denunciation for capital crimes suffers from the same defect. If capital crimes require the punishment of death in order to provide moral reinforcement for the basic values of the community, those values can only be undermined when death is so rarely inflicted upon the criminals who commit the crimes. Furthermore, it is certainly doubtful that the infliction of death by the State does in fact strengthen the community's moral code; if the deliberate extinguishment of human life has any effect at all, it more likely tends to lower our respect for life and brutalize our values. That, after all, is why we no longer carry out public executions. In any event, this claim simply means that one purpose of punishment is to indicate social disapproval of crime. To serve that purpose our laws distribute punishments according to the gravity of crimes and punish more severely the crimes society regards as more serious. That purpose cannot justify any particular punishment as the upper limit of severity.

There is, then, no substantial reason to believe that the punishment of death, as currently administered, is necessary for the protection of society. The only other purpose suggested, one that is independent of protection for society, is retribution. Shortly stated, retribution in this context means that criminals are put to death because they deserve it.

Although it is difficult to believe that any State today wishes to proclaim adherence to 'naked vengeance' [*Trop v.*

Dulles], the States claim, in reliance upon its statutory authorization, that death is the only fit punishment for capital crimes and that this retributive purpose justifies its infliction. In the past, judged by its statutory authorization, death was considered the only fit punishment for the crime of forgery, for the first federal criminal statute provided a mandatory death penalty for that crime. Obviously, concepts of justice change; no immutable moral order requires death for murderers and rapists. The claim that death is a just punishment necessarily refers to the existence of certain public beliefs. The claim must be that for capital crimes death alone comports with society's notion of proper punishment. As administered today, however, the punishment of death cannot be justified as a necessary means of exacting retribution from criminals. When the overwhelming number of criminals who commit capital crimes go to prison, it cannot be concluded that death serves the purpose of retribution more effectively than imprisonment. The asserted public belief that murderers and rapists deserve to die is flatly inconsistent with the execution of a random few. As the history of the punishment of death in this country shows, our society wishes to prevent crime; we have no desire to kill criminals simply to get even with them.

Death Is Therefore Cruel and Unusual

In sum, the punishment of death is inconsistent with all four principles: Death is an unusually severe and degrading punishment; there is a strong probability that it is inflicted arbitrarily; its rejection by contemporary society is virtually total; and there is no reason to believe that it serves any penal purpose more effectively than the less severe punishment of imprisonment. The function of these principles is to enable a court to determine whether a punishment comports with human dignity. Death, quite simply, does not.

The Death Penalty's Constitutionality Is Restored

Potter Stewart

Just four years after *Furman v. Georgia*, in which the Supreme Court declared that the death penalty was "wantonly" and "freakishly" imposed and therefore unconstitutional, *Gregg v. Georgia* came before the Court. Troy Gregg was charged with committing armed robbery and murder. Upon sentencing, the trial judge outlined specific circumstances that must be met in order for the jury to return a sentence of death; the crime committed indeed met two of the three circumstances outlined by the judge, and the death verdict was returned. Gregg appealed. In the majority opinion written by Potter Stewart, the Court determined that while the procedures previously used to administer the death penalty had been unconstitutional, the penalty itself was not. Therefore, once proper assurances were made to prevent the misuse of the penalty (in this case, the aggravating circumstances as outlined by the trial judge), states were once again free to implement it. This ruling resulted in the resumption of executions in many states. Stewart served on the Supreme Court from 1959 to 1981.

We address initially the basic contention that the punishment of death for the crime of murder is, under all circumstances, "cruel and unusual" in violation of the Eighth and Fourteenth Amendments of the Constitution. . . .

The Court on a number of occasions has both assumed and asserted the constitutionality of capital punishment. In

Potter Stewart, majority opinion, *Gregg v. Georgia*, 428 U.S. 153, 1976.

several cases that assumption provided a necessary foundation for the decision, as the Court was asked to decide whether a particular method of carrying out a capital sentence would be allowed to stand under the Eighth Amendment. But until *Furman v. Georgia* [1972], the Court never confronted squarely the fundamental claim that the punishment of death always, regardless of the enormity of the offense or the procedure followed in imposing the sentence, is cruel and unusual punishment in violation of the Constitution. Although this issue was presented and addressed in *Furman*, it was not resolved by the Court. Four Justices would have held that capital punishment is not unconstitutional *per se*; two Justices would have reached the opposite conclusion; and three Justices, while agreeing that the statutes then before the Court were invalid as applied, left open the question whether such punishment may ever be imposed. We now hold that the punishment of death does not invariably violate the Constitution.

The Early History of the Eighth Amendment

The history of the prohibition of "cruel and unusual" punishment already has been reviewed at length. The phrase first appeared in the English Bill of Rights of 1689, which was drafted by Parliament at the accession of William and Mary. . . . The English version appears to have been directed against punishments unauthorized by statute and beyond the jurisdiction of the sentencing court, as well as those disproportionate to the offense involved. The American draftsmen, who adopted the English phrasing in drafting the Eighth Amendment, were primarily concerned, however, with proscribing "tortures" and other "barbarous" methods of punishment.

In the earliest cases raising Eighth Amendment claims, the Court focused on particular methods of execution to determine whether they were too cruel to pass constitutional muster. The constitutionality of the sentence of death itself was not at issue, and the criterion used to evaluate the mode of execution was its similarity to "torture" and other "barbarous" methods [*Wilkerson v. Utah* (1879)]. . . .

A Flexible and Dynamic Amendment

But the Court has not confined the prohibition embodied in the Eighth Amendment to "barbarous" methods that were generally outlawed in the 18th century. Instead the Amendment has been interpreted in a flexible and dynamic manner. The Court early recognized that "a principle to be vital, must be capable of wider application than the mischief which gave it birth" [*Weems v. United States* (1910)]. Thus the Clause forbidding "cruel and unusual" punishments "is not fastened to the obsolete but may acquire meaning as public opinion becomes enlightened by a humane justice" [*Weems*].

In *Weems* the Court addressed the constitutionality of the Philippine punishment of *Cadena temporal* for the crime of falsifying an official document. That punishment included imprisonment for at least 12 years and one day, in chains, at hard and painful labor; the loss of many basic civil rights; and subjection to lifetime surveillance. Although the Court acknowledged the possibility that "the cruelty of pain" may be present in the challenged punishment, it did not rely on that factor, for it rejected the proposition that the Eighth Amendment reaches only punishments that are "inhuman and barbarous, torture and the like." Rather, the Court focused on the lack of proportion between the crime and the offense:

> Such penalties for such offenses amaze those who have formed their conception of the relation of a state to even its offending citizens from the practice of the American commonwealths, and believe that it is a precept of justice that punishment for crime should be graduated and proportioned to offense.

Later, in *Trop v. Dulles* [1958], the Court reviewed the constitutionality of the punishment of denationalization imposed upon a soldier who escaped from an Army stockade and became a deserter for one day. Although the concept of proportionality was not the basis of the holding, the plurality observed . . . that "(f)ines, imprisonment and even execution may be imposed depending upon the enormity of the crime."

The substantive limits imposed by the Eighth Amendment on what can be made criminal and punished were discussed in *Robinson v. California* [1962]. The Court found unconstitutional a state statute that made the status of being addicted to a narcotic drug a criminal offense. It held, in effect, that it is "cruel and unusual" to impose any punishment at all for the mere status of addiction. The cruelty in the abstract of the actual sentence imposed was irrelevant: "Even one day in prison would be a cruel and unusual punishment for the 'crime' of having a common cold." Most recently, in *Furman v. Georgia,* . . . three Justices in separate concurring opinions found the Eighth Amendment applicable to procedures employed to select convicted defendants for the sentence of death.

It is clear from the foregoing precedents that the Eighth Amendment has not been regarded as a static conce. As Mr. Chief Justice Warren said, in an oft-quoted phrase, "(t)he Amendment must draw its meaning from the evolving standards of decency that mark the progress of a maturing society" [*Trop v. Dulles* (1958)]. Thus, an assessment of contemporary values concerning the infliction of a challenged sanction is relevant to the application of the Eighth Amendment. As we develop below more fully, this assessment does not call for a subjective judgment. It requires, rather, that we look to objective indicia that reflect the public attitude toward a given sanction.

Amendment Eight and "the Dignity of Man"

But our cases also make clear that public perceptions of standards of decency with respect to criminal sanctions are not conclusive. A penalty also must accord with "the dignity of man," which is the "basic concept underlying the Eighth Amendment" [*Trop v. Dulles* (1958)]. This means, at least, that the punishment not be "excessive." When a form of punishment in the abstract (in this case, whether capital punishment may ever be imposed as a sanction for murder) rather than in the particular (the propriety of death as a penalty to be applied to a specific defendant for a specific crime) is under consideration, the inquiry into "excessiveness" has two aspects. First, the punishment must not involve the unnecessary and wanton infliction of pain. Second,

the punishment must not be grossly out of proportion to the
severity of the crime.

The Eighth Amendment as a Restraint of Power

Of course, the requirements of the Eighth Amendment must
be applied with an awareness of the limited role to be played
by the courts. This does not mean that judges have no role to
play, for the Eighth Amendment is a restraint upon the exercise of legislative power. . . .

But, while we have an obligation to insure that constitutional bounds are not overreached, we may not act as judges
as we might as legislators. . . .

Therefore, in assessing a punishment selected by a demo-
cratically elected legislature against the constitutional measure,
we presume its validity. We may not require the legislature to
select the least severe penalty possible so long as the penalty
selected is not cruelly inhumane or disproportionate to the
crime involved. And a heavy burden rests on those who would
attack the judgment of the representatives of the people. . . .

Past Rulings Support the Death Penalty

In the discussion to this point we have sought to identify the
principles and considerations that guide a court in addressing
an Eighth Amendment claim. We now consider specifically
whether the sentence of death for the crime of murder is a Per
se violation of the Eighth and Fourteenth Amendments to the
Constitution. We note first that history and precedent
strongly support a negative answer to this question.

The imposition of the death penalty for the crime of murder has a long history of acceptance both in the United States
and in England. The common-law rule imposed a mandatory
death sentence on all convicted murderers. And the penalty
continued to be used into the 20th century by most American
States, although the breadth of the common-law rule was diminished, initially by narrowing the class of murders to be
punished by death and subsequently by widespread adoption
of laws expressly granting juries the discretion to recommend
mercy.

It is apparent from the text of the Constitution itself that the existence of capital punishment was accepted by the Framers. At the time the Eighth Amendment was ratified, capital punishment was a common sanction in every State. Indeed, the First Congress of the United States enacted legislation providing death as the penalty for specified crimes. The Fifth Amendment, adopted at the same time as the Eighth, contemplated the continued existence of the capital sanction by imposing certain limits on the prosecution of capital cases:

> No person shall be held to answer for a capital, or otherwise infamous crime, unless on a presentment or indictment of a Grand Jury . . . ; nor shall any person be subject for the same offense to be twice put in jeopardy of life or limb; . . . nor be deprived of life, liberty, or property, without due process of law. . . .

And the Fourteenth Amendment, adopted over three-quarters of a century later, similarly contemplates the existence of the capital sanction in providing that no State shall deprive any person of "life, liberty, or property" without due process of law.

For nearly two centuries, this Court, repeatedly and often expressly, has recognized that capital punishment is not invalid Per se. In *Wilkerson v. Utah* [1879], where the Court found no constitutional violation in inflicting death by public shooting, it said:

> Cruel and unusual punishments are forbidden by the Constitution, but the authorities referred to are quite sufficient to show that the punishment of shooting as a mode of executing the death penalty for the crime of murder in the first degree is not included in that category, within the meaning of the eighth amendment.

Rejecting the contention that death by electrocution was "cruel and unusual," the Court reiterated:

> The punishment of death is not cruel, within the meaning of that word as used in the Constitution. It implies there something inhuman and barbarous, something

more than the mere extinguishment of life [*In re Kemmler*, 1890].

Again, in *Louisiana ex rel. Francis v. Resweber* [1947], the Court remarked: "The cruelty against which the Constitution protects a convicted man is cruelty inherent in the method of punishment, not the necessary suffering involved in any method employed to extinguish life humanely." And in *Trop v. Dulles* [1958], Mr. Chief Justice Warren, for himself and three other Justices, wrote:

> Whatever the arguments may be against capital punishment, both on moral grounds and in terms of accomplishing the purposes of punishment . . . the death penalty has been employed throughout our history, and, in a day when it is still widely accepted, it cannot be said to violate the constitutional concept of cruelty.

Society's Response to the *Furman* Ruling

Four years ago, the petitioners in *Furman* and its companion cases predicated their argument primarily upon the asserted proposition that standards of decency had evolved to the point where capital punishment no longer could be tolerated. The petitioners in those cases said, in effect, that the evolutionary process had come to an end, and that standards of decency required that the Eighth Amendment be construed finally as prohibiting capital punishment for any crime regardless of its depravity and impact on society. This view was accepted by two Justices. Three other Justices were unwilling to go so far; focusing on the procedures by which convicted defendants were selected for the death penalty rather than on the actual punishment inflicted, they joined in the conclusion that the statutes before the Court were constitutionally invalid.

The petitioners in the capital cases before the Court today renew the "standards of decency" argument, but developments during the four years since *Furman* have undercut substantially the assumptions upon which their argument rested. Despite the continuing debate, dating back to the 19th century, over the morality and utility of capital punishment, it is now evident that a large proportion of American society continues to regard it as an appropriate and necessary criminal sanction.

The most marked indication of society's endorsement of the death penalty for murder is the legislative response to *Furman*. The legislatures of at least 35 States have enacted new statutes that provide for the death penalty for at least some crimes that result in the death of another person. And the Congress of the United States, in 1974, enacted a statute providing the death penalty for aircraft piracy that results in death. These recently adopted statutes have attempted to address the concerns expressed by the Court in *Furman*. Primarily (i) by specifying the factors to be weighed and the procedures to be followed in deciding when to impose a capital sentence, or (ii) by making the death penalty mandatory for specified crimes. But all of the post-*Furman* statutes make clear that capital punishment itself has not been rejected by the elected representatives of the people. . . .

The Role of the Jury

The jury also is a significant and reliable objective index of contemporary values because it is so directly involved. The Court has said that "one of the most important functions any jury can perform in making . . . a selection (between life imprisonment and death for a defendant convicted in a capital case) is to maintain a link between contemporary community values and the penal system" [*Witherspoon v. Illinois* (1968)]. It may be true that evolving standards have influenced juries in recent decades to be more discriminating in imposing the sentence of death. But the relative infrequency of jury verdicts imposing the death sentence does not indicate rejection of capital punishment Per se. Rather, the reluctance of juries in many cases to impose the sentence may well reflect the humane feeling that this most irrevocable of sanctions should be reserved for a small number of extreme cases. . . .

The Purpose of the Death Penalty

As we have seen, however, the Eighth Amendment demands more than that a challenged punishment be acceptable to contemporary society. The Court also must ask whether it comports with the basic concept of human dignity at the core of the Amendment. Although we cannot "invalidate a category of penalties because we deem less severe penalties adequate to serve the ends of penology" [*Furman v. Georgia* (1972)], the sanction imposed cannot be so totally without penological justification that it results in the gratuitous infliction of suffering.

The death penalty is said to serve two principal social purposes: retribution and deterrence of capital crimes by prospective offenders.

In part, capital punishment is an expression of society's moral outrage at particularly offensive conduct. This function may be unappealing to many, but it is essential in an ordered society that asks its citizens to rely on legal processes rather than self-help to vindicate their wrongs.

> The instinct for retribution is part of the nature of man, and channeling that instinct in the administration of criminal justice serves an important purpose in promoting the stability of a society governed by law. When people begin to believe that organized society is unwilling or unable to impose upon criminal offenders the punishment they "deserve," then there are sown the seeds of anarchy of self-help, vigilante justice, and lynch law [*Furman v. Georgia*].

"Retribution is no longer the dominant objective of the criminal law" [*Williams v. New York* (1949)] but neither is it a forbidden objective nor one inconsistent with our respect for the dignity of men. Indeed, the decision that capital punishment may be the appropriate sanction in extreme cases is an expression of the community's belief that certain crimes are themselves so grievous an affront to humanity that the only adequate response may be the penalty of death.

The Death Penalty as a Deterrent

Statistical attempts to evaluate the worth of the death penalty as a deterrent to crimes by potential offenders have occasioned a great deal of debate. The results simply have been inconclusive. . . .

Although some of the studies suggest that the death penalty may not function as a significantly greater deterrent than lesser penalties, there is no convincing empirical evidence either supporting or refuting this view. We may nevertheless assume safely that there are murderers, such as those who act in passion, for whom the threat of death has little or no deterrent effect. But for many others, the death penalty undoubtedly is a significant deterrent. There are carefully contemplated murders, such as murder for hire, where the possible penalty of death may well enter into the cold calculus that precedes the decision to act. And there are some categories of murder, such as murder by a life prisoner, where other sanctions may not be adequate.

The value of capital punishment as a deterrent of crime is a complex factual issue the resolution of which properly rests with the legislatures, which can evaluate the results of statistical studies in terms of their own local conditions and with a flexibility of approach that is not available to the courts. Indeed, many of the post-*Furman* statutes reflect just such a responsible effort to define those crimes and those criminals for which capital punishment is most probably an effective deterrent.

The Death Penalty Is Not Unconstitutional Per Se

In sum, we cannot say that the judgment of the Georgia Legislature that capital punishment may be necessary in some cases is clearly wrong. Considerations of federalism, as well as respect for the ability of a legislature to evaluate, in terms of its particular State, the moral consensus concerning the death penalty and its social utility as a sanction, require us to conclude, in the absence of more convincing evidence, that the infliction of death as a punishment for murder is not without justification and thus is not unconstitutionally severe.

Finally, we must consider whether the punishment of death is disproportionate in relation to the crime for which it is imposed. There is no question that death as a punishment is unique in its severity and irrevocability. When a defendant's life is at stake, the Court has been particularly sensitive to insure that every safeguard is observed. But we are concerned here only with the imposition of capital punishment for the crime of murder, and when a life has been taken deliberately by the offender, we cannot say that the punishment is invariably disproportionate to the crime. It is an extreme sanction, suitable to the most extreme of crimes.

We hold that the death penalty is not a form of punishment that may never be imposed, regardless of the circumstances of the offense, regardless of the character of the offender, and regardless of the procedure followed in reaching the decision to impose it.

Supreme Court Rulings After *Furman* and *Gregg* Have Created Confusion

Stuart Banner

After the *Gregg v. Georgia* (1976) ruling reinstated the death penalty, the application of the penalty was called into question in a variety of instances. The result was a barrage of Eighth Amendment cases before the Supreme Court. In the following excerpt, Stuart Banner summarizes the post-*Gregg* Supreme Court rulings on the death penalty. Such rulings addressed which crimes warranted the death penalty and whether juveniles or the mentally challenged should be executed. He concludes that the Court's rulings have created a complex and inconsistent body of law regarding capital punishment. Stuart Banner is a professor of law at Washington University in St. Louis.

Capital punishment after *Gregg* [*v. Georgia*, 1976] was not just a political issue. The Supreme Court's involvement turned it into a constitutional issue as well, one that returned to the Court year after year. Within a very short time the Court constructed an intricate Eighth Amendment jurisprudence on the foundation of *Furman* [*v. Georgia*, 1972] and *Gregg*, a body of cases distinguishing the practices that would or would not amount to cruel and unusual punishment. The result was a significant shift in decisionmaking authority among the three branches of government. The various issues involving the death penalty that had once been decided by legislatures, or by governors during the clemency

Stuart Banner, *The Death Penalty: An American History.* Cambridge, MA: Harvard University Press, 2002. Copyright © 2002 by the President and Fellows of Harvard College. Reproduced by permission.

process, now became constitutional questions to be decided by courts.

Only Murder Is Punishable by Death

For instance, was capital punishment disproportionately severe for crimes less grave than murder? The question had been the subject of fierce political debate within legislatures since the late eighteenth century. Governors had always considered the gravity of the crime in deciding whether to grant clemency. But after *Furman* and *Gregg* the issue was recast as a constitutional question: Would it violate the Eighth Amendment to execute a criminal for committing a crime short of murder? In *Coker v. Georgia*, only a year after *Gregg*, the Court held that the death penalty was a cruel and unusual punishment for rape. Every death sentence imposed for the rest of the century would be for murder. But what about a defendant technically guilty of murder who was not the actual killer? The criminal law had always held accomplices guilty of the crime they helped another commit, but a defendant's minimal participation had always been a factor tending toward clemency. Now it became a constitutional question: Was it cruel and unusual to execute the accomplice? In 1982 the Court held that it was, by a 5-4 vote; in 1987, after Justice [Byron] White switched sides, the Court held that it was not, also by a 5-4 vote [*Enmund v. Florida*, 1982; *Tison v. Arizona*, 1987].

Who Is Subject to the Death Penalty?

Just about every death penalty question that had once been decided by legislatures in enacting statutes or by governors in ruling on clemency petitions was addressed by the Supreme Court in the years after *Gregg*. What if the defendant was very young? The Court held that the Eighth Amendment permitted the execution of a defendant who was sixteen years old at the time he committed the crime. What if the defendant had become insane by the time of the execution? The Court held that the Eighth Amendment prohibited executing the insane. What if the defendant was mentally retarded? The Court held that the Eighth Amendment did not prohibit executing the retarded. These had been classic legislative or clemency issues for hundreds of years, but now they were novel constitutional questions. The ultimate issue on clemency was of course whether the defendant was in fact innocent, and it was only a matter of time before that too became a constitutional question. Was it cruel and unusual punishment to execute an innocent person? *Herrera v. Collins*, the 1993 case that posed the question, produced five separate opinions and no clear answer. *Furman* and *Gregg* had the effect of moving some very old questions into a new forum.

Clarifying Eligibility for the Death Penalty

The constitutionalization of capital punishment produced a host of *new* questions as well. Some of the states' aggravating circumstances turned out to be so vague as to raise doubts that they provided any guidance to the jury. Georgia, for instance, authorized the death penalty for every murder the jury found "outrageously or wantonly vile, horrible or inhuman," a category that might not have excluded any murders at all. The same could have been said about one of Oklahoma's aggravating circumstances, that the murder be "especially heinous, atrocious or cruel." The Court found both aggravating circumstances unconstitutional. A few years later, however, the Court approved an aggravating circumstance adopted by Idaho, that in committing the murder the defendant "exhibited utter disregard for human life." That too might easily be said about all murders, but because the Idaho courts interpreted "utter disregard" to refer only to what they called "the cold-blooded, pitiless slayer," the Court found that the aggravating circumstance adequately distinguished one category of murders from another [*Godfrey v. Georgia*, 1980; *Maynard v. Cartwright*, 1988; *Arave v. Creech*, 1993]. It was in the interest of death penalty supporters to draft aggravating circumstances that pulled in as many murders as possible, so the Court found itself repeatedly examining whether particular circumstances sufficiently confined the jury's discretion to impose the death sentence.

Supporters of the death penalty had the opposite interest with respect to mitigating circumstances. There the incentive was to draft statutes narrowly, to *exclude* as many murders as possible. This practice also produced repeated constitutional challenges. In the end the Court held that the states could not restrict the jury's consideration of mitigating evidence—that the jury must be allowed to consider any kind of evidence that might point against a death sentence, not just the evidence relevant to one of the statutory mitigating circumstances [*Lockett v. Ohio*, 1978; *Eddings v. Oklahoma*, 1982]. That conclusion went halfway toward undermining the constitutional regime created by *Furman* and *Gregg*, under which state statutes were supposed to channel the jury's consideration of evidence at sentencing to prevent the random imposition of death sentences. If the constitution instead required juries to consider *any* mitigating evidence, half the decision was unguided.

Most of the other half of the decision, the identification of aggravating circumstances, was cut loose from statutory guidance not long after, when the Court allowed sentencing juries to consider nonstatutory aggravating evidence as well. By this point all that was left of the constitutional framework was the requirement that the jury find a single statutory aggravating circumstance before proceeding to what had become a virtually unguided exercise of discretion. And even that threshold requirement was generally acknowledged as something of a sham, because as time went on sentencing statutes were typically expanded to include aggravating circumstances phrased so broadly as to exclude very few murders. Missouri's statute, for example, included as aggravating circumstances that the murder evidenced "depravity of mind," that the murder was committed in the course of another felony or to conceal another felony, and that the murderer hoped he or a confederate would obtain some of the victim's property [*Zant v. Stephens*, 1983]. It was a rare murder for which an applicable aggravating circumstance could not be found, which meant that at sentencing just about any kind of evidence could be introduced for either side and considered by jurors any way they wanted.

For a time the Court did exclude one kind of evidence from sentencing, evidence of the effect of the murder on the victim's family and friends, but that was by a 5-4 vote. In 1991, after [Justice William J.] Brennan retired and was replaced by David Souter, the Court overruled its prior cases and let in such "victim impact evidence" as well [*Payne v. Tennessee*, 1991]. After 1991 well-conducted capital sentencing hearings normally included emotional presentations by both sides, matching the defendant's weeping relatives against the victim's weeping relatives, in an effort to gain the sympathy of the jury. Any pretense that this was a rational process of distinguishing degrees of culpability was long gone.

The Eighth Amendment "Fog of Confusion"

In the twenty years after *Gregg* capital punishment occupied a significant percentage of the Court's time, resulting in scores of cases that made up a complex and ever-shifting body of law. Justice Antonin Scalia, among other critics, complained of "the fog of confusion that is our annually improvised Eighth Amendment, 'death is different' jurisprudence." Much of the fog was produced by the Court's constant effort to reconcile two irreconcilable goals—consistency across cases (a goal best reached by formal rules restricting jury discretion) and attention to the unique characteristics of each case (a goal best reached by allowing the jury unrestricted discretion). In 1994, a few months before he retired, Harry Blackmun finally gave up and decided the death penalty ought to be unconstitutional under all circumstances. "Over the past two decades, efforts to balance these competing constitutional commands have been to no avail," he despaired. "From this day forward, I no longer shall tinker with the machinery of death." Lewis Powell came to the same conclusion a few years after his retirement, when his opinion no longer made any difference. But the rest of the Court tinkered on.

Many areas of the law are complex, but the tragedy of the Court's Eighth Amendment jurisprudence was that all the complexity served scarcely any purpose. Trials were long and expensive, lawyers had to master bodies of arcane doctrine, every case raised several issues that could be plausibly litigated on appeal, and yet, for all that, the process of distinguishing the murderers who would be executed from those who would be sent to prison seemed no less haphazard than it had been before the Supreme Court got involved. Lawyers and trial judges went through the motions, but in the end juries imposed death virtually for whatever reasons they chose. There was little dispute that the purpose behind *Furman* and *Gregg*, to use the Constitution to rationalize capital sentencing, had not been achieved. Critics on the right complained that the Court's Eighth Amendment jurisprudence forced state governments to spend time and money for no good purpose; critics on the left complained that the Court had watered *Furman* down to irrelevance. Both sides were right.

The Constitution Authorizes the Death Penalty

Ernest van den Haag

In the following excerpt Ernest van den Haag asserts that the death penalty is constitutional in light of the Eighth, Fifth, and Fourteenth Amendments. Van den Haag first concedes that under the Eighth Amendment punishments must mesh with society's evolving standards (as ruled in the Supreme Court case *Trop v. Dulles*, 1958). However, he insists that this fact does not render the punishment unconstitutional. He points out that because the Constitution specifically refers to the deprivation of life under the Fifth Amendment, the penalty is authorized. To declare the penalty unconstitutional, without altering the Constitution itself, would render the Constitution a superfluous and meaningless document. Next, he states that both discrimination and "chanciness" are always factors in upholding the law, so it is unfair to single out capital punishment alone for abolition on these grounds. Finally, van den Haag states that proportionality, or the idea that similar crimes should receive similar punishments, is not a constitutional guarantee. Therefore, arguments that the penalty should be abolished because not all murders result in a death sentence should be disregarded. Van den Haag is a proponent of the death penalty and has written numerous books and articles on the subject.

The fifth amendment, passed in 1791, states that "no person shall be deprived of life, liberty, or property, without due process of law." Thus, with "due process of law," the

Ernest van den Haag, "The Death Penalty Once More," *University of California–Davis Law Review*, vol. 18, Summer 1985, pp. 957–64.

Constitution authorizes depriving persons "of life, liberty or property." The fourteenth amendment, passed in 1868, applies an identical provision to the states. The Constitution, then, authorizes the death penalty. It is left to elected bodies to decide whether or not to retain it.

The eighth amendment, reproducing almost verbatim a passage from the English Bill of Rights of 1689, prohibits "cruel and unusual punishments." This prohibition was not meant to repeal the fifth amendment since the amendments were passed simultaneously. "Cruel" punishment is not prohibited unless "unusual" as well, that is, new, rare, not legislated, or disproportionate to the crime punished. Neither the English Bill of Rights, nor the eighth amendment, hitherto has been found inconsistent with capital punishment.

Evolving Standards Do Not De-Authorize Death

Some commentators argue that, in *Trop v. Dulles* [1958], the Supreme Court indicated that "evolving standards of decency that mark the progress of a maturing society" allow courts to declare "cruel and unusual," punishments authorized by the Constitution. However, *Trop* was concerned with expatriation, a punishment that is not specifically authorized by the Constitution. The death penalty is. *Trop* did not suggest that "evolving standards" could de-authorize what the Constitution repeatedly authorizes. Indeed, Chief Justice [Earl] Warren, writing for the majority in *Trop*, declared that "the death penalty . . . cannot be said to violate the constitutional concept of cruelty." Furthermore, the argument based on "evolving standards" is paradoxical: the Constitution would be redundant if current views, enacted by judicial *fiat*, could supersede what it plainly says. If "standards of decency" currently invented or evolved could, without formal amendment, replace or repeal the standards authorized by the Constitution, the Constitution would be superfluous.

It must be remembered that the Constitution does not force capital punishment on the population but merely authorizes it. Elected bodies are left to decide whether to use the authorization. As for "evolving standards," how could courts detect them without popular consensus as a guide? Moral revelations accepted by judges, religious leaders, sociologists, or academic elites, but not by the majority of voters, cannot suffice. The opinions of the most organized, most articulate, or most vocal might receive unjustified deference. Surely the eighth amendment was meant to limit, but was not meant to replace, decisions by the legislative branch, or to enable the judiciary to do what the voters won't do. The general consensus on which the courts would have to rely could be registered only by elected bodies. They favor capital punishment. Indeed, at present, more than seventy percent of the voters approve of the death penalty. The state legislatures reflect as much. Wherefore, the Supreme Court, albeit reluctantly, rejected abolition of the death penalty by judicial *fiat*. This decision was subsequently qualified by a finding that the death penalty for rape is disproportionate to the crime, and by rejecting all mandatory capital punishment.

There Will Always Be Chanciness in Capital Punishment

Laws that allowed courts too much latitude to decide, perhaps capriciously, whether to actually impose the death penalty in capital cases also were found unconstitutional [*Furman v. Georgia*, 1972]. In response, more than two-thirds of the states have modified their death penalty statutes, listing aggravating and mitigating factors, and imposing capital punishment only when the former outweigh the latter. The Supreme Court is satisfied that this procedure meets the constitutional requirements of non-capriciousness [*Gregg v. Georgia*, 1976]. However, abolitionists are not.

In *Capital Punishment: The Inevitability of Caprice and Mistake*, Professor Charles Black contends that the death penalty is necessarily imposed capriciously, for irremediable reasons. If he is right, he has proved too much, unless capital punishment is imposed more capriciously now than it was in 1791 or 1868, when the fifth and fourteenth amendments were enacted. He does not contend that it is. Professor Black also stresses that the elements of chance, unavoidable in all penalizations, are least tolerable when capital punishment is involved. But the irreducible chanciness inherent in human efforts does not constitutionally require the abolition of capital punishment, unless the framers were less aware of chance and human frailty than Professor Black is. . . .

Considering Discrimination and the Death Penalty

Sociologists have demonstrated that the death penalty has been distributed in a discriminatory pattern in the past: black or poor defendants were more likely to be executed than equally guilty others. This argues for correction of the distributive process, but not for abolition of the penalty it distributes, unless constitutionally excessive maldistribution ineluctably inheres in the penalty. There is no evidence to that effect. Actually, although we cannot be sure that it has disappeared altogether, discrimination has greatly decreased compared to the past.

However, recently the debate on discrimination has taken a new turn. Statistical studies have found that, *ceteris paribus* [all things being equal], a black man who murders a white has a much greater chance to be executed than he would have had, had his victim been black. This discriminates against black *victims* of murder: they are not as fully, or as often, vindicated as are white victims. However, although unjustified per se, discrimination against a class of victims need not, and here does not, amount to discrimination against their victimizers. The pattern discriminates *against* black murderers of whites and *for* black murderers of blacks. One may describe it as discrimination for, or discrimination against, just as one may describe a glass of water as half full or half empty. Discrimination against one group (here, blacks who kill whites) is necessarily discrimination in favor of another (here, blacks who kill blacks).

Most black victims are killed by black murderers, and a disproportionate number of murder victims is black. Wherefore the discrimination in favor of murderers of black victims more than offsets, numerically, any remaining discrimination against other black murderers.

Comparative Excessiveness: Equality and Justice Are Not the Same

Recently lawyers have argued that the death penalty is unconstitutionally disproportionate if defendants, elsewhere in the state, received lesser sentences for comparable crimes. But the Constitution only requires that penalties be appropriate to the gravity of the crime, not that they cannot exceed penalties imposed elsewhere. Although some states have adopted "comparative excessiveness" reviews, there is no constitutional requirement to do so.

Unavoidably, different courts, prosecutors, defense lawyers, judges and juries produce different penalties even when crimes seem comparable. Chance plays a great role in human affairs. Some offenders are never caught or convicted, while others are executed; some are punished more than others guilty of worse crimes. Thus, a guilty person, or group of persons, may get away with no punishment, or with a light punishment, while others receive the punishment they deserve. Should we let these others go too, or punish them less severely? Should we abolish the penalty applied unequally or discriminatorily?

The late Justice [William O.] Douglas [in *Furman*] suggested an answer to these questions:

> A law that . . . said that blacks, those who never went beyond the fifth grade in school, those who made less than $3,000 a year, or those who were unpopular or unstable should be the only people executed [would be wrong]. A law which in the overall view reaches that result in practice has no more sanctity than a law which in terms provides the same.

Justice Douglas' answer here conflates an imagined discriminatory law with the discriminatory application of a non-discriminatory law. His imagined law would be inconsistent with the "equal protection of the laws" demanded by the fourteenth amendment, and the Court would have to invalidate it *ipso facto*. But discrimination caused by uneven application of non-discriminatory death penalty laws may be remedied by means other than abolition, as long as the discrimination is not intrinsic to the laws.

Consider now, albeit fleetingly, the moral as distinguished from the constitutional bearing of discrimination. Suppose guilty defendants are justly executed, but only if poor, or black and not otherwise. This unequal justice would be morally offensive for what may be called tautological reasons. If any punishment for a given crime is just, then a greater or lesser punishment is not. Only one punishment can be just for all persons equally guilty of the same crime. Therefore, different punishments for equally guilty persons or group members are unjust: some offenders are punished more than they deserve, or others less.

Still, equality and justice are not the same. "Equal justice" is not a redundant phrase. Rather, we strive for two distinct ideals, justice and equality. Neither can replace the other. We want to have justice and, having it, we want to extend it equally to all. We would not want equal injustice. Yet, sometimes, we must choose between equal injustice and unequal justice. What should we prefer? Unequal justice is justice still, even if only for some, whereas equal injustice is injustice for all. If not every equally guilty person is punished equally, we have unequal justice. It seems preferable to equal injustice—having no guilty person punished as deserved. Since it is never possible to punish equally all equally guilty murderers, we should punish, as they deserve, as many of those we apprehend and convict as possible. Thus, even if the death penalty were inherently discriminatory—which is not the case—but deserved by those who receive it, it would be morally just to impose it on them. If, as I contend, capital punishment is just and not inherently discriminatory, it remains desirable to eliminate inequality in distribution, to apply the penalty to all who deserve it, sparing no racial or economic class. But if a guilty person or group escaped the penalty through our porous system, wherein is this an argument for sparing others?

If one does not believe capital punishment can be just, discrimination becomes a subordinate argument, since one would object to capital punishment even if it were distributed equally to all the guilty. If one does believe that capital punishment for murderers is deserved, discrimination against guilty black murderers and in favor of equally guilty white murderers is wrong, not because blacks receive the deserved punishment, but because whites escape it.

Consider a less emotionally charged analogy. Suppose traffic police ticketed all drivers who violated the rules, except drivers of luxury cars. Should we abolish tickets? Should we decide that the ticketed drivers of nonluxury cars were unjustly punished and ought not to pay their fines? Would they become innocent of the violation they are guilty of because others have not been ticketed? Surely the drivers of luxury cars should not be exempted. But the fact that they were is no reason to exempt drivers of nonluxury cars as well. Laws could never be applied if the escape of one person, or group, were accepted as grounds for not punishing another. To do justice is primarily to punish as deserved, and only secondarily to punish equally.

Guilt is personal. No one becomes less guilty or less deserving of punishment because another was punished leniently or not at all. That justice does not catch up with all guilty persons understandably is resented by those caught. But it does not affect their guilt. If some, or all, white and rich murderers escape the death penalty, how does that reduce the guilt of black or poor murderers, or make them less deserving of punishment, or deserving of a lesser punishment?

Some lawyers have insisted that the death penalty is distributed among those guilty of murder as though by a lottery and that the worst may escape it. They exaggerate, but suppose one grants the point. How do those among the guilty selected for execution by lottery become less deserving of punishment because others escaped it? What is wrong is that these others escaped, not that those among the guilty who were selected by the lottery did not.

Those among the guilty actually punished by a criminal justice system unavoidably are selected by chance, not because we want to so select them, but because the outcome of our efforts largely depends on chance. No murderer is punished unless he is unlucky enough both to be caught and to have convinced a court of his guilt. And courts consider evidence not truth. They find truth only when the evidence establishes it.

Thus they may have reasonable doubts about the guilt of an actually guilty person. Although we may strive to make justice as equal as possible, unequal justice will remain our lot in this world. We should not give up justice, or the death penalty, because we cannot extend it as equally to all the guilty as we wish. If we were not to punish one offender because another got away because of caprice or discrimination, we would give up justice for the sake of equality. We would reverse the proper order of priorities.

Executing Mentally Retarded Persons Is Cruel and Unusual Punishment

John Paul Stevens

Daryl Renard Atkins was convicted of abduction, armed robbery, and capital murder for a crime committed in 1996. In the penalty phase of the trial, it was revealed that Atkins was mildly mentally retarded, with an IQ of fifty-nine. The Virginia jury sentenced him to death, but the penalty was overturned by the Supreme Court in 2002. The Court's decision was based in part on its determination that society had become increasingly opposed to executing the mentally retarded; it stated as evidence the number of states that had previously banned these executions through their legislatures. In addition, the Court noted that mentally retarded individuals are less culpable, therefore undeserving of the ultimate punishment, and that executing mentally retarded persons serves no deterrent effect. *Atkins v. Virginia* is considered a landmark case because it marked a significant shift in the Supreme Court's view of the death penalty in the era following *Gregg v. Georgia* (1976), the case that reinstated the penalty. *Atkins* thereby opened the door for similar cases, such as those opposing the execution of mentally ill persons and juveniles. It will likely be used as a precedent in arguing against these practices. John Paul Stevens has served on the Supreme Court since 1975.

Those mentally retarded persons who meet the law's requirements for criminal responsibility should be tried

John Paul Stevens, majority opinion, *Atkins v. Virginia,* 536 U.S. 304, 2002.

and punished when they commit crimes. Because of their disabilities in areas of reasoning, judgment, and control of their
impulses, however, they do not act with the level of moral
culpability that characterizes the most serious adult criminal conduct. Moreover, their impairments can jeopardize the
reliability and fairness of capital proceedings against mentally retarded defendants. Presumably for these reasons, in
the 13 years since we decided *Penry* v. *Lynaugh* [1989] the
American public, legislators, scholars, and judges have delib-
erated over the question whether the death penalty should
ever be imposed on a mentally retarded criminal. The consensus reflected in those deliberations informs our answer to
the question presented by this case: whether such executions
are "cruel and unusual punishments" prohibited by the
Eighth Amendment to the Federal Constitution.

The Details of *Atkins* v. *Virginia*

Petitioner, Daryl Renard Atkins, was convicted of abduction,
armed robbery, and capital murder, and sentenced to death. . . .

In the penalty phase, the defense relied on one witness,
Dr. Evan Nelson, a forensic psychologist who had evaluated
Atkins before trial and concluded that he was "mildly mentally retarded." His conclusion was based on interviews with
people who knew Atkins, a review of school and court records,
and the administration of a standard intelligence test which
indicated that Atkins had a full scale IQ of 59.

The jury sentenced Atkins to death. . . .

The Supreme Court of Virginia affirmed the imposition of
the death penalty. Atkins did not argue before the Virginia
Supreme Court that his sentence was disproportionate to
penalties imposed for similar crimes in Virginia, but he did
contend "that he is mentally retarded and thus cannot be
sentenced to death." The majority of the state court rejected
this contention, relying on our holding in *Penry*. The Court
was "not willing to commute Atkins' sentence of death to life
imprisonment merely because of his IQ score."

[Virginia Supreme Court] Justice [Leroy Rountree] Has-
sell and [Virginia Supreme Court] Justice [Lawrence L.]
Koontz dissented. They rejected Dr. [Stanton] Samenow's

opinion that Atkins possesses average intelligence as "incredulous as a matter of law," and concluded that "the imposition of the sentence of death upon a criminal defendant who has the mental age of a child between the ages of 9 and 12 is excessive." In their opinion, "it is indefensible to conclude that individuals who are mentally retarded are not to some degree less culpable for their criminal acts. By definition, such individuals have substantial limitations not shared by the general population. A moral and civilized society diminishes itself if its system of justice does not afford recognition and consideration of those limitations in a meaningful way.". . .

The Eighth Amendment and Proportionality

The Eighth Amendment succinctly prohibits "excessive" sanctions. It provides: "Excessive bail shall not be required, nor excessive fines imposed, nor cruel and unusual punishments inflicted." In *Weems* v. *United States* [1910], we held that a punishment of 12 years jailed in irons at hard and painful labor for the crime of falsifying records was excessive. We explained "that it is a precept of justice that punishment for crime should be graduated and proportioned to the offense." We have repeatedly applied this proportionality precept in later cases interpreting the Eighth Amendment. [See *Harmelin* v. *Michigan* (1991).] Thus, even though "imprisonment for ninety days is not, in the abstract, a punishment which is either cruel or unusual," it may not be imposed as a penalty for "the 'status' of narcotic addiction" [*Robinson* v. *California* (1962)] because such a sanction would be excessive. As Justice [Potter] Stewart explained in *Robinson*: "Even one day in prison would be a cruel and unusual punishment for the 'crime' of having a common cold."

A claim that punishment is excessive is judged not by the standards that prevailed in 1685 when Lord Jeffreys presided over the "Bloody Assizes" or when the Bill of Rights was adopted, but rather by those that currently prevail. As Chief Justice [Earl] Warren explained in his opinion in *Trop* v. *Dulles* [1958]: "The basic concept underlying the Eighth Amendment is nothing less than the dignity of man. . . . The Amendment must draw its meaning from the evolving standards of decency that mark the progress of a maturing society."

Proportionality review under those evolving standards should be informed by "'objective factors to the maximum possible extent,'" [see *Harmelin*, quoting *Rummel* v. *Estelle* (1980)] We have pinpointed that the "clearest and most reliable objective evidence of contemporary values is the legislation enacted by the country's legislatures" [*Penry*]. Relying in part on such legislative evidence, we have held that death is an impermissibly excessive punishment for the rape of an adult woman [*Coker* v. *Georgia* (1977)] or for a defendant who neither took life, attempted to take life, nor intended to take life [*Enmund* v. *Florida* (1982)]. . . .

We . . . acknowledged in *Coker* that the objective evidence, though of great importance, did not "wholly determine" the controversy, "for the Constitution contemplates that in the end our own judgment will be brought to bear on the question of the acceptability of the death penalty under the Eighth Amendment." For example, in *Enmund*, we concluded by expressing our own judgment about the issue:

> For purposes of imposing the death penalty, Enmund's criminal *culpability* must be limited to his participation in the robbery, and his punishment must be tailored to his personal responsibility and moral guilt. Putting Enmund to death to avenge two killings that he did not commit and had no intention of committing or causing does not measurably contribute to the retributive end of ensuring that the criminal gets his just deserts. This is the judgment of most of *the legislatures that have recently addressed the matter, and we have no reason to disagree with that judgment* for purposes of construing and applying the Eighth Amendment (emphasis added).

Thus, in cases involving a consensus, our own judgment is "brought to bear" [*Coker*], by asking whether there is reason to disagree with the judgment reached by the citizenry and its legislators.

Guided by our approach in these cases, we shall first review the judgment of legislatures that have addressed the suitability of imposing the death penalty on the mentally retarded and then consider reasons for agreeing or disagreeing with their judgment.

Legislation Regarding the Execution of Mentally Retarded Persons

The parties have not called our attention to any state legislative consideration of the suitability of imposing the death penalty on mentally retarded offenders prior to 1986. In that year, the public reaction to the execution of a mentally retarded murderer [Jerome Bowden] in Georgia apparently led to the enactment of the first state statute prohibiting such executions. In 1988, when Congress enacted legislation reinstating the federal death penalty, it expressly provided that a "sentence of death shall not be carried out upon a person who is mentally retarded." In 1989, Maryland enacted a similar prohibition. It was in that year that we decided *Penry*, and concluded that those two state enactments, "even when added to the 14 States that have rejected capital punishment completely, do not provide sufficient evidence at present of a national consensus."

Much has changed since then. Responding to the national attention received by the Bowden execution and our decision in *Penry*, state legislatures across the country began to address the issue. In 1990 Kentucky and Tennessee enacted statutes similar to those in Georgia and Maryland, as did New Mexico in 1991, and Arkansas, Colorado, Washington, Indiana, and Kansas in 1993 and 1994. In 1995, when New York reinstated its death penalty, it emulated the Federal Government by expressly exempting the mentally retarded. Nebraska followed suit in 1998. There appear to have been no similar enactments during the next two years, but in 2000 and 2001 six more States—South Dakota, Arizona, Connecticut, Florida, Missouri, and North Carolina—joined the procession. The Texas Legislature unanimously adopted a similar bill, and bills have passed at least one house in other States, including Virginia and Nevada.

It is not so much the number of these States that is significant, but the consistency of the direction of change. Given the well-known fact that anticrime legislation is far more popular than legislation providing protections for persons guilty of violent crime, the large number of States prohibiting the execution of mentally retarded persons (and the complete absence of States passing legislation reinstating the power to conduct such executions) provides powerful evidence that today our society views mentally retarded offenders as categorically less culpable than the average criminal. The evidence carries even greater force when it is noted that the legislatures that have addressed the issue have voted overwhelmingly in favor of the prohibition. Moreover, even in those States that allow the execution of mentally retarded offenders, the practice is uncommon. Some States, for example New Hampshire and New Jersey, continue to authorize executions, but none have been carried out in decades. Thus there is little need to pursue legislation barring the execution of the mentally retarded in those States. And it appears that even among those States that regularly execute offenders and that have no prohibition with regard to the mentally retarded, only five have executed offenders possessing a known IQ less than 70 since we decided *Penry*. The practice, therefore, has become truly unusual, and it is fair to say that a national consensus has developed against it.

To the extent there is serious disagreement about the execution of mentally retarded offenders, it is in determining which offenders are in fact retarded. In this case, for instance, the Commonwealth of Virginia disputes that Atkins suffers from mental retardation. Not all people who claim to be mentally retarded will be so impaired as to fall within the range of mentally retarded offenders about whom there is a national consensus. As was our approach in *Ford* v. *Wainwright* [1986], with regard to insanity, "we leave to the State[s] the task of developing appropriate ways to enforce the constitutional restriction upon its execution of sentences."

Excluding the Mentally Retarded from the Death Penalty Is Appropriate

This consensus unquestionably reflects widespread judgment about the relative culpability of mentally retarded offenders, and the relationship between mental retardation and the penological purposes served by the death penalty. Additionally, it suggests that some characteristics of mental retardation undermine the strength of the procedural protections that our capital jurisprudence steadfastly guards. . . .

Clinical definitions of mental retardation require not only subaverage intellectual functioning, but also significant limitations in adaptive skills such as communication, self-care, and self-direction that became manifest before age 18. Mentally retarded persons frequently know the difference between right and wrong and are competent to stand trial. Because of their impairments, however, by definition they have diminished capacities to understand and process information, to communicate, to abstract from mistakes and learn from experience, to engage in logical reasoning, to control impulses, and to understand the reactions of others. There is no evidence that they are more likely to engage in criminal conduct than others, but there is abundant evidence that they often act on impulse rather than pursuant to a premeditated plan, and that in group settings they are followers rather than leaders. Their deficiencies do not warrant an exemption from criminal sanctions, but they do diminish their personal culpability.

In light of these deficiencies, our death penalty jurisprudence provides two reasons consistent with the legislative consensus that the mentally retarded should be categorically excluded from execution. First, there is a serious question as to whether either justification that we have recognized as a basis for the death penalty applies to mentally retarded offenders. *Gregg* v. *Georgia* identified "retribution and deterrence of capital crimes by prospective offenders" as the social purposes served by the death penalty. Unless the imposition of the death penalty on a mentally retarded person "measurably contributes to one or both of these goals, it 'is nothing more than the purposeless and needless imposition of pain and suffering,' and hence an unconstitutional punishment" [*Enmund*].

With respect to retribution—the interest in seeing that the offender gets his "just deserts"—the severity of the appropriate punishment necessarily depends on the culpability of the offender. Since *Gregg*, our jurisprudence has consistently confined the imposition of the death penalty to a narrow

category of the most serious crimes. For example, in *Godfrey*
v. *Georgia* [1980] we set aside a death sentence because the
petitioner's crimes did not reflect "a consciousness materially
more 'depraved' than that of any person guilty of murder." If
the culpability of the average murderer is insufficient to justify the most extreme sanction available to the State, the
lesser culpability of the mentally retarded offender surely
does not merit that form of retribution. Thus, pursuant to
our narrowing jurisprudence, which seeks to ensure that only
the most deserving of execution are put to death, an exclusion for the mentally retarded is appropriate.

Executing the Mentally Retarded Will Not Deter Others

With respect to deterrence—the interest in preventing capital
crimes by prospective offenders—"it seems likely that 'capital
punishment can serve as a deterrent only when murder is the
result of premeditation and deliberation'" [*Enmund*]. Exempting the mentally retarded from that punishment will not affect the "cold calculus that precedes the decision" of other
potential murderers [*Gregg*]. Indeed, that sort of calculus is
at the opposite end of the spectrum from behavior of mentally
retarded offenders. The theory of deterrence in capital sentencing is predicated upon the notion that the increased
severity of the punishment will inhibit criminal actors from
carrying out murderous conduct. Yet it is the same cognitive
and behavioral impairments that make these defendants less
morally culpable—for example, the diminished ability to understand and process information, to learn from experience,
to engage in logical reasoning, or to control impulses—that
also make it less likely that they can process the information
of the possibility of execution as a penalty and, as a result,
control their conduct based upon that information. Nor will
exempting the mentally retarded from execution lessen the
deterrent effect of the death penalty with respect to offenders
who are not mentally retarded. Such individuals are unpro-
tected by the exemption and will continue to face the threat of
execution. Thus, executing the mentally retarded will not
measurably further the goal of deterrence.

The Mentally Retarded Make Poor Defendants

The reduced capacity of mentally retarded offenders provides a second justification for a categorical rule making such offenders ineligible for the death penalty. The risk "that the death penalty will be imposed in spite of factors which may call for a less severe penalty" [*Lockett* v. *Ohio* (1978)] is enhanced, not only by the possibility of false confessions, but also by the lesser ability of mentally retarded defendants to make a persuasive showing of mitigation in the face of prosecutorial evidence of one or more aggravating factors. Mentally retarded defendants may be less able to give meaningful assistance to their counsel and are typically poor witnesses, and their demeanor may create an unwarranted impression of lack of remorse for their crimes. As *Penry* demonstrated, moreover, reliance on mental retardation as a mitigating factor can be a two-edged sword that may enhance the likelihood that the aggravating factor of future dangerousness will be found by the jury. Mentally retarded defendants in the aggregate face a special risk of wrongful execution.

Punishing the Mentally Retarded with Execution Is Excessive

Our independent evaluation of the issue reveals no reason to disagree with the judgment of "the legislatures that have recently addressed the matter" and concluded that death is not a suitable punishment for a mentally retarded criminal. We are not persuaded that the execution of mentally retarded criminals will measurably advance the deterrent or the retributive purpose of the death penalty. Construing and applying the Eighth Amendment in the light of our "evolving standards of decency," we therefore conclude that such punishment is excessive and that the Constitution "places a substantive restriction on the State's power to take the life" of a mentally retarded offender [*Ford*].

The judgment of the Virginia Supreme Court is reversed and the case is remanded for further proceedings not inconsistent with this opinion.

Executing Juveniles Should Be Deemed Cruel and Unusual Punishment

Adam Ortiz

After the *Atkins v. Virginia* (2002) ruling barred the execution of mentally retarded individuals, crusades to halt the executions of other subpopulations began. One of those crusades is the movement to ban the execution of juveniles. In this essay, Adam Ortiz contends that the arguments made in the *Atkins* case regarding the mentally retarded apply equally to the case of juveniles. For example, just as there is a trend among state legislatures to ban the execution of the mentally retarded, there is a similar trend to outlaw the execution of juveniles. In addition, similar to the mentally retarded, juveniles lack a completely developed mental capacity and thus are not completely culpable for their crimes. For these reasons and others, juvenile executions should be banned. Adam Ortiz is the Soros Criminal Justice Fellow at the American Bar Association's Juvenile Justice Center.

"Offenses committed by juveniles under the age of 18 do not merit the death penalty. The practice of executing such offenders is a relic of the past and is inconsistent with evolving standards of decency in a civilized society. We should put an end to this shameful practice."

In re Stanford (2002), J. Stevens, dissenting

This statement is among the most recent expressions of a divided U.S. Supreme Court that 14 years earlier nar-

Adam Ortiz, "Cruel and Unusual Punishment: The Juvenile Death Penalty: Evolving Standards of Decency," www.abanet.org, January 2004. Copyright © 2004 by The American Bar Association. Reproduced by permission.

rowly upheld the constitutionality of the right of states to execute juvenile offenders. Ironically, this recent dissent was in the case of Kevin Stanford, the same juvenile offender who was the petitioner in the 1989 case which ultimately upheld the constitutionality of executing 16 and 17-year-old offenders [*Stanford v. Kentucky* (1989)].

Since then, much has changed. This paper will outline these changes in light of the framework for evaluating Eighth Amendment claims that the Court established in *Atkins v. Virginia* [2002]. The *Atkins* Court considered the closely related issue of the death penalty for the mentally retarded, holding that a national consensus against executing the mentally retarded had evolved, and the practice was, therefore, unconstitutional. These two groups, juvenile offenders and mentally retarded offenders, have been deemed by . . . legal scholar [Victor L. Streib] the "Siamese twins" of the death penalty, their status inextricably linked in constitutional principle and substance.

The *Atkins* Framework

The *Atkins* opinion is launched from the touchstone of Eighth Amendment jurisprudence: Chief Justice [Earl] Warren's elegant axiom that "the Amendment must draw its meaning from the evolving standards of decency that mark the progress of a maturing society" [*Trop v. Dulles* (1958)].

These evolving standards of decency are to be measured by "objective factors to the maximum possible extent" [*Coker v. Georgia* (1977)]. These objective factors primarily include, in order of importance, (1) state legislation, (2) sentencing decisions of juries, and (3) the views of entities with relevant expertise.

In addition to these relatively measurable indicators, opinions from *Marbury v. Madison* [1803] to the present day establish that the Court may bring its own judgment to bear. In modern Eighth Amendment jurisprudence, the criteria for this judgment is outlined in *Gregg v. Georgia* [1976], which established that imposition of the death penalty should "serve two principal social purposes: retribution and deterrence."

Although there is agreement that the Court must consider objective factors, the Justices disagree as to what degree of these factors indicates a consensus (e.g. What is an appropriate number of states? Death convictions? Executions?) and how a balance is struck between these measurable indicia and the Court's judgment.

Based upon an examination of the objective factors and the Justices' own judgment, the *Atkins* Court found a consensus against the execution of the mentally retarded. Using this framework, a comparison of the evidence of an "evolving standard of decency" between these two classes of offenders, the mentally retarded and juveniles, finds the two issues virtually indistinguishable.

State Legislation on Executing Juveniles

In *Atkins*, the Court noted that 30 states had expressly prohibited the death penalty for the mentally retarded and declared that fact evidence of an evolving consensus. At the time of this report, 29 states prohibit the death penalty for juvenile offenders.

This is a reflection of state governments' steadily growing opposition to the punishment. In *Stanford v. Kentucky* (1989), a contentious 4-1-4 plurality concluded that state actions did not, at that time, indicate an evolving consensus.

Since *Stanford*, however, six states have banned the practice. Indiana abolished the juvenile death penalty in 2002, and Montana did the same in 1999. In both states, the legislation passed with a near-unanimous vote. When New York reinstated the death penalty in 1995, it rejected the juvenile death penalty and set the minimum age at 18, as Kansas had done in 1994. Finally, the Supreme Courts of Missouri and Washington State banned the practice in 2003 and 1993, respectively.

Other jurisdictions prohibiting the death penalty for those who committed crimes under the age of 18 are the District of Columbia, the federal government, and the U.S. Military.

States that do not have the death penalty on their books should also be included in determining a national consensus, since their legislatures have considered the issue and rejected capital punishment for all offenders, including minors.

In *Atkins*, the Court considered the laws of 30 states to be "powerful evidence that today our society views mentally retarded offenders as categorically less culpable than the average criminal."

A majority of these states had changed their laws regarding offenders with mental retardation in the preceding five years, a fact which incurred criticism from Justice [Antonin] Scalia. His *Atkins* dissent suggested that this "very recently enacted" legislation might be a passing fancy or fad. That argument does not apply to the trend of prohibiting juvenile executions. The 29 states that do not allow the juvenile death penalty have changed their laws over decades of steady deliberation.

The "Direction of Change"

In *Atkins*, the Court considered the importance of an issue's momentum: "It is not so much the number of these states that is significant, but the consistency of the direction of change."

Regarding juveniles, the direction is clear. Since *Stanford*, none of the 40 death penalty jurisdictions have passed legislation to lower the minimum age of eligibility for capital punishment to sixteen. This lack of action is significant. To use a related example, after *Gregg* established the guidelines for a constitutional death penalty standard, 38 states responded with new statutes, a reflection of a consensus for a death penalty. After *Stanford*, however, not a single state lowered its age of eligibility, despite receiving a green light to do so.

The *Atkins* plurality also took note of the three states that had passed legislation in only one chamber. The juvenile legislative record is more impressive in this regard: seven states have passed relevant legislation in one house since *Stanford*.

In 2002, the Texas House voted 72-42 to raise the age of eligibility to 18 (note that Texas is the only state that regularly carries out the executions of minors). The Florida Senate passed a bill in 2002 and 2001. The Arkansas Senate did so in 2002. In 2003, the Nevada Senate and South Dakota House passed a juvenile ban, and Missouri's Senate voted to raise the age of eligibility to 17. In New Hampshire, legislation was passed to abolish the death penalty completely in

2000, but the Governor vetoed it. In 2003, 14 states introduced legislation to ban the juvenile death penalty: AL, AR,
AZ, DE, FL, KY, MS, MO, NV, PA, OK, SD, TX, and WY. This
number represents more than half of the number of states
that allow the execution of juvenile offenders.

Clearly, states that retain the juvenile death penalty but
never use it have little incentive to pursue legislation ban-
ning it (a point raised in *Atkins* . . .). This argument has
greater force given that most state legislatures meet only for
a few months each year, and some only hold session every
other year. Likewise, there is little need for concerned organizations and members of the public to demand change, although support for such change appears to be high.

Juvenile Executions: Truly Unusual

Carrying out a juvenile execution has become a highly unusual occurrence. Of the 21 states that retain the death
penalty for juvenile offenders, only one has utilized it with
any frequency. Texas, having carried out 13 such executions
since the death penalty was reinstated, stands apart. Virginia
and Oklahoma follow distantly, having carried out three and
two executions, respectively. At the time of this writing, these
three states have carried out 82% of all executions of juvenile
offenders in the United States in the last 25 years.

Georgia, Louisiana, Missouri, and South Carolina have each
executed one juvenile offender since 1976. Prior to these modern day executions, Louisiana last executed a juvenile in 1948,
Georgia in 1957, Missouri in 1921, and South Carolina in 1948.
Oklahoma had never executed a juvenile offender prior to
1999. Clearly, the punishment is "unusual" in these states.

Nationwide, 43 states have not executed a juvenile offender, 39 have no juvenile offenders on death row, and five
states have two or less. Again, Texas outdistances all other
states with 28 juveniles facing death.

Courts and Juries on Juvenile Executions

The behavior of juries is a critical indicator nearly on par
with the actions of legislators. On this issue, trends in our
courts are compelling. The reversal rate for death sentences

imposed on juvenile offenders is an appalling 85%. Juries are also increasingly reluctant to impose death on a juvenile. In 2003, juvenile death sentences dropped to only 2% of the total number of death sentences imposed, part of a steady decline from a high of 5.3% in 1994.

Notably, a Virginia jury unanimously chose a life in prison sentence over the death penalty for juvenile "sniper" Lee Malvo. Not only did this Virginia jury, who was under no illusion as to the heinous nature of this crime, choose life over death for the youth, but an ABC News Poll released on December 14, 2003 found that a majority of Americans preferred to spare the life of Lee Malvo.

Taken together, these trends suggest reluctance among prosecutors, judges and jurors to impose and carry out juvenile death sentences.

What Entities with Expertise Say

The *Atkins* Court looked at "additional evidence [that] makes it clear that this legislative judgment reflects a much broader social and professional consensus," including organizations with relevant expertise.

Although Justice [William H.] Rehnquist dissented that "none should be accorded any weight," such organizations have historically served a critical function in the enlightenment of American society, a fact noted by Alexis de Tocqueville in 1840. Indeed, as a national resource of special knowledge and significant part of the collective American mind, referenced in countless endeavors throughout our society, these organizations of expertise were deemed worthy of the Court's consideration.

Explicit opposition to the execution of juvenile offenders by expert organizations has been longstanding, diverse, and continues to increase. Conversely, no such organization has taken a position in favor of executing minors.

Medical and health groups that oppose the juvenile death penalty include the American Association of Child and Adolescent Psychiatry, the American Academy of Pediatrics, the American Society for Adolescent Psychiatry, the American Psychiatric Association, the National Alliance for the Mentally

Ill, the National Association of Social Workers, and the National Mental Health Association. Child welfare organizations that oppose the practice include the Children's Defense Fund, the Child Welfare League of America, the Coalition for Juvenile Justice, the National Education Association and the Youth Law Center. Religious and ethical organizations include American Baptist Churches in the USA, the Catholic Bishops of the United States, the Episcopal Church, the Presbyterian Church, the Union of American Hebrew Congregations and the United Methodist Church. The American Bar Association has opposed the practice since 1983.

Notably, a blue-ribbon commission established by the Washington-based Constitution Project to examine the capital punishment system explicitly opposed the death penalty for juveniles in its final report, *Mandatory Justice*. The diversity and credentials of its members are striking and include supporters and opponents of the death penalty, Democrats and Republicans, conservatives and liberals, former judges, prosecutors, crime victims, and scholars.

What the American Public Thinks

Although not a primary indicator of a national consensus, the *Atkins* Court did reinforce its findings by examining public opinion research. Similar findings abound regarding the juvenile death penalty. A 2001 University of Chicago study found that while 62% support the death penalty in general, only 34% "favor it for those under age 18." Another study by Princeton Survey Research Associates showed that 72% favored the death penalty for serious murders, but only 38% wanted it applied to juveniles. Similarly, a May 2002 Gallup poll showed that 69% of Americans oppose executing juveniles, a level of opposition that has remained constant for 70 years.

Opinions Worldwide

The *Atkins* Court also considered international opinion. Worldwide, the execution of juvenile offenders has all but ended. In fact, the Inter-American Commission on Human Rights found that the U.S. is violating a *jus cogens* [a principle of international law based on fundamental values] norm of international law by executing juvenile offenders. In regard to codified international law, it is clearly prohibited by the International Covenant on Civil and Political Rights (ICCPR), the American Convention on Human Rights, and the U.N. Convention on the Rights of the Child (CRC). The United States and Somalia (which, according to the State Department, has not had a recognizable central government since 1991) are the only two countries (of 193) that have not yet ratified the CRC.

In the last ten years, the U.S. has executed more juvenile offenders (17) than all other nations combined (9), and with greater frequency. In the U.S., juvenile executions comprise approximately 4% of all executions in the last 10 years. However, for the rest of the world, juvenile executions comprise approximately .04% of all executions during the same time. Also, fewer nations are carrying out juvenile executions. Since 2000, four other countries in the world are known to have executed juveniles: China, Democratic Republic of Congo (DRC), Iran, and Pakistan. However, China's law forbids executing juveniles, Pakistan recently abolished the death penalty for juvenile offenders, and Iran has publicly stated that it does not use the punishment and intends to outlaw it.

A Parallel to *Atkins*: Executing Juveniles Should Be Prohibited

A look at the standards employed by the *Atkins* Court that rendered the execution of the mentally retarded unconstitutional, i.e. the actions of states, juries and entities with expertise, among other indicia, apply with comparable or greater force toward juveniles.

It is beyond the scope of this paper to examine the vast and growing body of scientific evidence supporting the assertion that juveniles cannot possess the level of maturity, reasoning, and judgment necessary to justify the ultimate punishment. Again, the parallels between the Court's considerations in *Atkins* justifying a categorical exemption for the mentally retarded and those of juveniles are clear; there is the higher possibility of false confessions, the lesser ability to give meaningful assistance to their counsel, and a special risk of wrongful execution.

CHAPTER THREE

What Forms of Punishment Are Cruel and Unusual?

The Bill of Rights

Divestment of Citizenship Violates the Eighth Amendment

Earl Warren

Divestment of citizenship is the stripping of citizenship from a naturally born citizen. In 1944 Albert Trop, a private in the U.S. Army, was divested of citizenship as punishment for desertion. Trop argued that this punishment was cruel and unusual and thereby violated the Eighth Amendment. The Supreme Court agreed in *Trop v. Dulles* (1958), stating that the divestment of citizenship should be reserved for the most extreme treasonous cases. Denationalization, the Court decreed, destroys an individual's status in organized society. This case became a benchmark as it declared that the basic purpose of the Eighth Amendment is nothing less than the preservation of human dignity. Earl Warren served as the chief justice of the Supreme Court from 1953 to 1969.

The petitioner in this case, a nativeborn American, is declared to have lost his United States citizenship and become stateless by reason of his conviction by court-martial for wartime desertion. As in *Perez v. Brownell* [1958], the issue before us is whether this forfeiture of citizenship comports with the Constitution.

The Facts of the Case

The facts are not in dispute. In 1944 petitioner was a private in the United States Army, serving in French Morocco. On May 22, he escaped from a stockade at Casablanca, where

Earl Warren, majority opinion, *Trop v. Dulles,* 356 U.S. 86, 1958.

he had been confined following a previous breach of discipline. The next day petitioner and a companion were walking along a road towards Rabat, in the general direction back to Casablanca, when an Army truck approached and stopped. A witness testified that petitioner boarded the truck willingly and that no words were spoken. In Rabat petitioner was turned over to military police. Thus ended petitioner's 'desertion.' He had been gone less than a day and had willingly surrendered to an officer on an Army vehicle while he was walking back towards his base. He testified that at the time he and his companion were picked up by the Army truck, 'we had decided to return to the stockade. The going was tough. We had no money to speak of, and at the time we were on foot and we were getting cold and hungry.' A general court-martial convicted petitioner of desertion and sentenced him to three years at hard labor, forfeiture of all pay and allowances and a dishonorable discharge.

In 1952 petitioner applied for a passport. His application was denied on the ground that under the provisions of Section 401(g) of the Nationality Act of 1940, as amended, he had lost his citizenship by reason of his conviction and dishonorable discharge for wartime desertion. In 1955 petitioner commenced this action in the District Court, seeking a declaratory judgment that he is a citizen. . . .

Section 401(g), the statute that decrees the forfeiture of this petitioner's citizenship, is based directly on a Civil War statute, which provided that a deserter would lose his 'rights of citizenship.' The meaning of this phrase was not clear. When the 1940 codification and revision of the nationality laws was prepared, the Civil War statute was amended to make it certain that what a convicted deserter would lose was nationality itself. In 1944 the statute was further amended to provide that a convicted deserter would lose his citizenship only if he was dismissed from the service or dishonorably discharged. At the same time it was provided that citizenship could be regained if the deserter was restored to active duty in wartime with the permission of the military authorities.

Though these amendments were added to ameliorate the harshness of the statute, their combined effect produces a result that poses far graver problems than the ones that were sought to be solved. Section 401(g) as amended now gives the military authorities complete discretion to decide who among convicted deserters shall continue to be Americans and who shall be stateless. By deciding whether to issue and execute a dishonorable discharge and whether to allow a deserter to reenter the armed forces, the military becomes the arbiter of citizenship. And the domain given to it by Congress is not as narrow as might be supposed. Though the crime of desertion is one of the most serious in military law, it is by no means a rare event for a soldier to be convicted of this crime. The elements of desertion are simply absence from duty plus the intention not to return. Into this category falls a great range of conduct, which may be prompted by a variety of motives— fear, laziness, hysteria or any emotional imbalance. The offense may occur not only in combat but also in training camps for draftees in this country. The Solicitor General informed the Court that during World War II, according to Army estimates, approximately 21,000 soldiers and airmen were convicted of desertion and given dishonorable discharges by the sentencing courts-martial and that about 7,000 of these were actually separated from the service and thus rendered stateless when the reviewing authorities refused to remit their dishonorable discharges. Over this group of men, enlarged by whatever the corresponding figures may be for the Navy and Marines, the military has been given the power to grant or withhold citizenship. And the number of youths subject to this power could easily be enlarged simply by expanding the statute to cover crimes other than desertion. For instance, a dishonorable discharge itself might in the future be declared to be sufficient to justify forfeiture of citizenship.

Three times in the past three years we have been confronted with cases presenting important questions bearing on the proper relationship between civilian and military authority in this country. A statute such as Section 401(g) raises serious issues in this area, but in our view of this case it is unnecessary to deal with those problems. We conclude that the judgment in this case must be reversed for the following reasons. . . .

The Deprivation of Citizenship Is Not a Weapon

It is my conviction that citizenship is not subject to the general powers of the National Government and therefore cannot be divested in the exercise of those powers. The right may be voluntarily relinquished or abandoned either by express language or by language and conduct that show a renunciation of citizenship.

Under these principles, this petitioner has not lost his citizenship. Desertion in wartime, though it may merit the ultimate penalty, does not necessarily signify allegiance to a foreign state. Section 401(g) is not limited to cases of desertion to the enemy, and there is no such element in this case. This soldier committed a crime for which he should be and was punished, but he did not involve himself in any way with a foreign state. There was no dilution of his allegiance to this country. The fact that the desertion occurred on foreign soil is of no consequence. The Solicitor General acknowledged that forfeiture of citizenship would have occurred if the entire incident had transpired in this country.

Citizenship is not a license that expires upon misbehavior. The duties of citizenship are numerous, and the discharge of many of these obligations is essential to the security and well-being of the Nation. The citizen who fails to pay his taxes or to abide by the laws safeguarding the integrity of elections deals a dangerous blow to his country. But could a citizen be deprived of his nationality for evading these basic responsibilities of citizenship? In time of war the citizen's duties include not only the military defense of the Nation but also a full participation in the manifold activities of the civilian ranks. Failure to perform any of these obligations may cause the Nation serious injury, and, in appropriate circumstances, the punishing power is available to deal with derelictions of duty. But citizenship is not lost every time a duty of citizenship is shirked. And the deprivation of citizenship is not a weapon that the Government may use to express its displeasure at a citizen's conduct, however reprehensible that conduct may be. As long as a person does not voluntarily renounce or abandon his citizenship, and this petitioner has done neither, I believe his fundamental right of citizenship is secure. On this ground alone the judgment in this case should be reversed. . . .

The Evolving Standards of Decency

Section 401(g) is a penal law, and we must face the question whether the Constitution permits the Congress to take away citizenship as a punishment for crime. If it is assumed that the power of Congress extends to divestment of citizenship, the problem still remains as to this statute whether denationalization is a cruel and unusual punishment within the meaning of the Eighth Amendment. Since wartime desertion is punishable by death, there can be no argument that the penalty of denationalization is excessive in relation to the gravity of the crime. The question is whether this penalty subjects the individual to a fate forbidden by the principle of civilized treatment guaranteed by the Eighth Amendment.

At the outset, let us put to one side the death penalty as an index of the constitutional limit on punishment. Whatever the arguments may be against capital punishment, both on moral grounds and in terms of accomplishing the purposes of punishment—and they are forceful—the death penalty has been employed throughout our history, and, in a day when it is still widely accepted, it cannot be said to violate the constitutional concept of cruelty. But it is equally plain that the existence of the death penalty is not a license to the Government to devise any punishment short of death within the limit of its imagination.

The exact scope of the constitutional phrase 'cruel and unusual' has not been detailed by this Court. But the basic policy reflected in these words is firmly established in the Anglo-American tradition of criminal justice. The phrase in our Constitution was taken directly from the English Declaration of Rights of 1688, and the principle it represents can be traced back to the Magna Carta. The basic concept underlying the Eighth Amendment is nothing less than the dignity of man. While the State has the power to punish, the Amendment stands to assure that this power be exercised within the limits of civilized standards. Fines, imprisonment and even execution may be imposed depending upon the enormity of the crime, but any technique outside the bounds of these traditional penalties is constitutionally suspect. This Court has had little occasion to give precise content to the Eighth Amendment, and, in an enlightened democracy such as ours, this is not surprising. But when the Court was confronted with a punishment of 12 years in irons at hard and painful labor imposed for the crime of falsifying public records, it did not hesitate to declare that the penalty was cruel in its excessiveness and unusual in its character [*Weems v. United States* (1910)]. The Court recognized in that case that the words of the Amendment are not precise, and that their scope is not static. The Amendment must draw its meaning from the evolving standards of decency that mark the progress of a maturing society.

Denationalization Is Barred by the Eighth Amendment

We believe . . . that use of denationalization as a punishment is barred by the Eighth Amendment. There may be involved no physical mistreatment, no primitive torture. There is instead the total destruction of the individual's status in organized society. It is a form of punishment more primitive than torture, for it destroys for the individual the political existence that was centuries in the development. The punishment strips the citizen of his status in the national and international political community. His very existence is at the sufferance of the country in which he happens to find himself. While any one country may accord him some rights, and presumably as long as he remained in this country he would enjoy the limited rights of an alien, no country need do so because he is stateless. Furthermore, his enjoyment of even the limited rights of an alien might be subject to termination at any time by reason of deportation. In short, the expatriate has lost the right to have rights.

This punishment is offensive to cardinal principles for which the Constitution stands. It subjects the individual to a fate of ever-increasing fear and distress. He knows not what discriminations may be established against him, what proscriptions may be directed against him, and when and for what cause his existence in his native land may be terminated. He may be subject to banishment, a fate universally decried by civilized people. He is stateless, a condition deplored in the international community of democracies. It is no answer to suggest that all the disastrous consequences of this fate may not be brought to bear on a stateless person. The threat makes the punishment obnoxious.

The civilized nations of the world are in virtual unanimity that statelessness is not to be imposed as punishment for crime. It is true that several countries prescribe expatriation in the event that their nationals engage in conduct in derogation of native allegiance. Even statutes of this sort are generally applicable primarily to naturalized citizens. But use of denationalization as punishment for crime is an entirely different matter. The United Nations' survey of the nationality laws of 84 nations of the world reveals that only two countries, the Philippines and Turkey, impose denationalization as a penalty for desertion. In this country the Eighth Amendment forbids that to be done.

The Gravity of Contradicting Legislation

In concluding as we do that the Eighth Amendment forbids Congress to punish by taking away citizenship, we are mindful of the gravity of the issue inevitably raised whenever the constitutionality of an Act of the National Legislature is challenged. No member of the Court believes that in this case the statute before us can be construed to avoid the issue of constitutionality. That issue confronts us, and the task of resolving it is inescapably ours. This task requires the exercise of judgment, not the reliance upon personal preferences. Courts must not consider the wisdom of statutes but neither can they sanction as being merely unwise that which the Constitution forbids.

We are oath-bound to defend the Constitution. This obligation requires that congressional enactments be judged by the standards of the Constitution. The Judiciary has the duty of implementing the constitutional safeguards that protect individual rights. When the Government acts to take away the fundamental right of citizenship, the safeguards of the Constitution should be examined with special diligence.

The provisions of the Constitution are not time-worn adages or hollow shibboleths. They are vital, living principles that authorize and limit governmental powers in our Nation. They are the rules of government. When the constitutionality of an Act of Congress is challenged in this Court, we must apply those rules. If we do not, the words of the Constitution become little more than good advice.

When it appears that an Act of Congress conflicts with one of these provisions, we have no choice but to enforce the paramount commands of the Constitution. We are sworn to do no less. We cannot push back the limits of the Constitution merely to accommodate challenged legislation. We must apply those limits as the Constitution prescribes them, bearing in mind both the broad scope of legislative discretion and the ultimate responsibility of constitutional adjudication. We do well to approach this task cautiously, as all our predecessors have counseled. But the ordeal of judgment cannot be shirked. In some 81 instances since this Court was established it has determined that congressional action exceeded the bounds of the Constitution. It is so in this case.

The judgment of the Court of Appeals for the Second Circuit is reversed and the cause is remanded to the District Court for appropriate proceedings.

The Eighth Amendment Does Not Guarantee Proportionate Sentencing

Antonin Scalia

Ronald Allen Harmelin was convicted of cocaine possession and was sentenced to life in prison without the possibility of parole. He appealed, arguing that the sentence was cruel and unusual for two reasons: first, that the sentence was disproportionate to the crime he committed; and second, that the judge had been required by Michigan law to impose such a sentence without considering the circumstances of the crime. The Supreme Court in *Harmelin v. Michigan* (1991) determined that some of its prior rulings had been wrong and that the Eighth Amendment includes no proportionality guarantee; that is, the Eighth Amendment does not guarantee that similar crimes will receive punishments that are proportionate in degree of severity. In the following excerpt from the Court's opinion, Antonin Scalia explains that the decision is based on the fact that proportionality is subjective, that it is difficult to assess the gravity of a crime and to compare "similarly grave" offenses, and that the process of comparing sentences between states is complex and often impossible. Harmelin's life sentence without the possibility for parole was therefore upheld. Antonin Scalia has served on the Supreme Court since 1986.

Petitioner [Ronald Allen Harmelin] was convicted of possessing 672 grams of cocaine and sentenced to a mandatory term of life in prison without possibility of parole. The

Antonin Scalia, majority opinion, *Harmelin v. Michigan,* 501 U.S. 957, 1991.

Michigan Court of Appeals initially reversed his conviction because evidence supporting it had been obtained in violation of the Michigan Constitution. On petition for rehearing, the Court of Appeals vacated its prior decision and affirmed petitioner's sentence, rejecting his argument that the sentence was "cruel and unusual" within the meaning of the Eighth Amendment. . . .

Petitioner claims that his sentence is unconstitutionally "cruel and unusual" for two reasons: first, because it is "significantly disproportionate" to the crime he committed; second, because the sentencing judge was statutorily required to impose it, without taking into account the particularized circumstances of the crime and of the criminal.

The History of Proportionality in the Court

The Eighth Amendment, which applies against the State by virtue of the Fourteenth Amendment, provides: "Excessive bail shall not be required, nor excessive fines imposed, nor cruel and unusual punishments inflicted." In *Rummel v. Estelle* [1980], we held that it did not constitute "cruel and unusual punishment" to impose a life sentence, under a recidivist statute, upon a defendant who had been convicted, successively, of fraudulent use of a credit card to obtain $80 worth of goods or services, passing a forged check in the amount of $28.36, and obtaining $120.75 by false pretenses. We said that "one could argue without fear of contradiction by any decision of this Court that for crimes concededly classified and classifiable as felonies, that is, as punishable by significant terms of imprisonment in a state penitentiary, the length of the sentence actually imposed is purely a matter of legislative prerogative." We specifically rejected the proposition asserted by the dissent (opinion of Powell, J.) that unconstitutional disproportionality could be established by weighing three factors: (1) gravity of the offense compared to severity of the penalty, (2) penalties imposed within the same jurisdiction for similar crimes, and (3) penalties imposed in other jurisdictions for the same offense. A footnote in the opinion, however, said: "This is not to say that a proportionality principle would not come into play in the extreme example mentioned by the dissent, . . . if a legislature made overtime parking a felony punishable by life imprisonment."

Two years later, in *Hutto v. Davis* [1982], we similarly rejected an Eighth Amendment challenge to a prison term of 40 years and fine of $20,000 for possession and distribution of approximately nine ounces of marijuana. We thought that result so clear in light of *Rummel* that our *per curiam* [by the court as a whole] opinion said the Fourth Circuit, in sustaining the constitutional challenge, "could be viewed as having ignored, consciously or unconsciously, the hierarchy of the federal court system," which could not be tolerated "unless we wish anarchy to prevail." And we again explicitly rejected application of the three factors discussed in the *Rummel* dissent. . . .

A year and a half after *Davis* we uttered what has been our last word on this subject to date. *Solem v. Helm* [1983], set aside under the Eighth Amendment, because it was disproportionate, a sentence of life imprisonment without possibility of parole, imposed under a South Dakota recidivist statute for successive offenses that included three convictions of third-degree burglary, one of obtaining money by false pretenses, one of grand larceny, one of third-offense driving while intoxicated, and one of writing a "no account" check with intent to defraud. . . .

Having decreed that a general principle of disproportionality exists [in the footnote discussing overtime parking in *Robinson*, which was later referred to in *Davis*] the Court used as the criterion for its application the three-factor test that had been explicitly rejected in both *Rummel* and *Davis*. . . .

Our 5-to-4 decision eight years ago in *Solem* was scarcely the expression of clear and well accepted constitutional law. . . . Accordingly, we have addressed anew, and in greater detail, the question whether the Eighth Amendment contains a proportionality guarantee—with particular attention to the background of the Eighth Amendment . . . and to the understanding of the Eighth Amendment before the end of the 19th century. . . . We conclude from this examination that *Solem* was simply wrong; the Eighth Amendment contains no proportionality guarantee. . . .

Proportionality Is Subjective

We think it enough that those who framed and approved the Federal Constitution chose, for whatever reason, not to include within it the guarantee against disproportionate sentences that some State Constitutions contained. It is worth noting, however, that there was good reason for that choice— a reason that reinforces the necessity of overruling *Solem.* While there are relatively clear historical guidelines and accepted practices that enable judges to determine which *modes* of punishment are "cruel and unusual," *proportionality* does not lend itself to such analysis. Neither Congress nor any state legislature has ever set out with the objective of crafting a penalty that is "disproportionate"; yet . . . many enacted dispositions seem to be so—because they were made for other times or other places, with different social attitudes, different criminal epidemics, different public fears, and different prevailing theories of penology. This is not to say that there are no absolutes; one can imagine extreme examples that no rational person, in no time or place, could accept. But for the same reason these examples are easy to decide, they are certain never to occur. The real function of a constitutional proportionality principle, if it exists, is to enable judges to evaluate a penalty that *some* assemblage of men and women *has* considered proportionate—and to say that it is not. For that real-world enterprise, the standards seem so inadequate that the proportionality principle becomes an invitation to imposition of subjective values.

The Difficulty of Assessing Gravity

This becomes clear, we think, from a consideration of the three factors that *Solem* found relevant to the proportionality determination: (1) the inherent gravity of the offense, (2) the sentences imposed for similarly grave offenses in the same jurisdiction, and (3) sentences imposed for the same crime in other jurisdictions. As to the first factor: Of course some offenses, involving violent harm to human beings, will always and everywhere be regarded as serious, but that is only half the equation. The issue is *what else* should be regarded to be *as serious* as these offenses, or even to be *more serious* than some of them. On that point, judging by the statutes that Americans have enacted, there is enormous variation—even within a given age, not to mention across the many generations ruled by the Bill of Rights. The State of Massachusetts punishes sodomy more severely than assault and battery, . . . whereas in several States, sodomy is not unlawful *at all*. In Louisiana, one who assaults another with a dangerous weapon faces the same maximum prison term as one who removes a shopping basket "from the parking area or grounds of any store . . . without authorization." A battery that results in "protracted and obvious disfigurement" merits imprisonment "for not more than five years," one half the maximum penalty for theft of livestock or an oilfield seismograph. We may think that the First Congress punished with clear disproportionality when it provided up to seven years in prison and up to $1,000 in fine for "cut[ting] off the ear or ears, . . . cut[ting] out or disabl[ing] the tongue, . . . put[ting] out an eye, . . . cut[ting] off . . . any limb or member of any person with intention . . . to maim or disfigure," but provided the death penalty for "run[ning] away with [a] ship or vessel, or any goods or merchandise to the value of fifty dollars." But then perhaps the citizens of 1791 would think that today's Congress punishes with clear disproportionality when it sanctions "assault by . . . wounding" with up to six months in prison, unauthorized reproduction of the "Smokey Bear" character or name with the same penalty, offering to barter a migratory bird with up to two years in prison, and purloining a "key suited to any lock adopted by the Post Office Department" with a prison term of up to 10 years. Perhaps both we and they would be right, but the point is that there are no textual or historical standards for saying so.

The difficulty of assessing gravity is demonstrated in the very context of the present case: Petitioner acknowledges that a mandatory life sentence might not be "grossly excessive" for possession of cocaine with intent to distribute [see *Hutto v. Davis* (1982)]. But surely whether it is a "grave" offense merely to possess a significant quantity of drugs—thereby facilitating distribution, subjecting the holder to the temptation of distribution, and raising the possibility of theft by others who might distribute—depends entirely upon how odious and socially threatening one believes drug use to be. Would it be "grossly excessive" to provide life imprisonment for "mere possession" of a certain quantity of heavy weaponry? If not, then the only issue is whether the possible dissemination of drugs can be as "grave" as the possible dissemination of heavy weapons. Who are we to say no? The members of the Michigan Legislature, and not we, know the situation on the streets of Detroit.

The Difficulty of Comparing "Similarly Grave" Offenses

The second factor suggested in *Solem* fails for the same reason. One cannot compare the sentences imposed by the jurisdiction for "similarly grave" offenses if there is no objective standard of gravity. Judges will be comparing what *they* consider comparable. Or, to put the same point differently: When it happens that two offenses judicially determined to be "similarly grave" receive significantly *dis* similar penalties, what follows is not that the harsher penalty is unconstitutional, but merely that the legislature does not share the judges' view that the offenses are similarly grave. Moreover, even if "similarly grave" crimes could be identified, the penalties for them would not necessarily be comparable, since there are many other justifications for a difference. For example, since deterrent effect depends not only upon the amount of the penalty but upon its certainty, crimes that are less grave but significantly more difficult to detect may warrant substantially higher penalties. Grave crimes of the sort that will not be deterred by penalty may warrant substantially lower penalties, as may grave crimes of the sort that are normally committed once in a lifetime by otherwise law-abiding citizens who will not profit from rehabilitation. Whether these differences will occur, and to what extent, depends, of course, upon the weight the society accords to deterrence and rehabilitation, rather than retribution, as the objective of criminal punishment (which is an eminently legislative judgment). In fact, it becomes difficult even to speak intelligently of "proportionality," once deterrence and rehabilitation are given significant weight. Proportionality is inherently a retributive concept, and perfect proportionality is the talionic law. . . .

The Difficulty of Comparing State-to-State Sentences

As for the third factor mentioned by *Solem*—the character of the sentences imposed by other States for the same crime—it must be acknowledged that that can be applied with clarity and ease. The only difficulty is that it has no conceivable relevance to the Eighth Amendment. That a State is entitled to treat with stern disapproval an act that other States punish with the mildest of sanctions follows *a fortiori* from the undoubted fact that a State may criminalize an act that other States do not criminalize *at all*. Indeed, a State may criminalize an act that other States choose to *reward*—punishing, for example, the killing of endangered wild animals for which other States are offering a bounty. What greater disproportion could there be than that? "Absent a constitutionally imposed uniformity inimical to traditional notions of federalism, some State will always bear the distinction of treating particular offenders more severely than any other State" [*Rummel*]. Diversity not only in policy, but in the means of implementing policy, is the very *raison d'être* of our federal system. Though the different needs and concerns of other States may induce them to treat simple possession of 672 grams of cocaine as a relatively minor offense, . . . nothing in the Constitution requires Michigan to follow suit. The Eighth Amendment is not a ratchet, whereby a temporary consensus on leniency for a particular crime fixes a permanent constitutional maximum, disabling the States from giving effect to altered beliefs and responding to changed social conditions.

A Certain Degree of Proportionality Must Exist

Our 20th-century jurisprudence has not remained entirely in accord with the proposition that there is no proportionality requirement in the Eighth Amendment, but neither has it departed to the extent that *Solem* suggests. In *Weems v.*

United States [1910] a government disbursing officer convicted of making false entries of small sums in his account
book was sentenced by Philippine courts to 15 years of *cadena temporal*. That punishment, based upon the Spanish
Penal Code called for incarceration at "hard and painful
labor" with chains fastened to the wrists and ankles at all
times. Several "accessor[ies]" were superadded, including
permanent disqualification from holding any position of public trust, subjection to "[government] surveillance" for life,
and "civil interdiction," which consisted of deprivation of "the
rights of parental authority, guardianship of person or property, participation in the family council [etc.]."

Justice [Joseph] McKenna, writing for himself and three
others, held that the imposition of *cadena temporal* was
"Cruel and Unusual Punishment." (Justice [Edward D.]
White, joined by Justice [Oliver W.] Holmes, dissented.) That
holding, and some of the reasoning upon which it was based,
was not at all out of accord with the traditional understanding of the provision we have described above. The punishment
was both (1) severe *and* (2) unknown to Anglo-American tradition. As to the former, Justice McKenna wrote:

> No circumstance of degradation is omitted. It may be
> that even the cruelty of pain is not omitted. He must
> bear a chain night and day. He is condemned to painful
> as well as hard labor. What painful labor may mean we
> have no exact measure. It must be something more
> than hard labor. It may be hard labor pressed to the
> point of pain.

As to the latter:

> It has no fellow in American legislation. Let us remem-
> ber that it has come to us from a government of a differ-
> ent form and genius from ours. It is cruel in its excess
> of imprisonment and that which accompanies and fol-
> lows imprisonment. It is unusual in its character.

Other portions of the opinion, however, suggest that mere
disproportionality, by itself, might make a punishment cruel
and unusual:

Such penalties for such offenses amaze those who . . . believe that it is a precept of justice that punishment for crime should be graduated and proportioned to offense.

The inhibition [of the Cruel and Unusual Punishments Clause] was directed, not only against punishments which inflict torture, "but against all punishments which by their excessive length or severity are greatly disproportioned to the offenses charged." [*Weems*] *O'Neil v. Vermont* (1892).

Disproportionate Must Equal "Barbaric" or "Excessive"

Since it contains language that will support either theory, our later opinions have used *Weems*, as the occasion required, to represent either the principle that "the Eighth Amendment bars not only those punishments that are 'barbaric' but also those that are 'excessive' in relation to the crime committed" [*Coker v. Georgia* (1977)] or the principle that only a "unique . . . punishmen[t]," a form of imprisonment different from the "more traditional forms . . . imposed under the Anglo-Saxon system," can violate the Eighth Amendment [*Rummel*]. If the proof of the pudding is in the eating, however, it is hard to view *Weems* as announcing a constitutional requirement of proportionality, given that it did not produce a decision implementing such a requirement, either here or in the lower federal courts, for six decades. In *Graham v. West Virginia* [1912], for instance, we evaluated (and rejected) a claim that life imprisonment for a third offense of horse theft was "cruel and unusual." We made no mention of *Weems*, although the petitioner had relied upon that case.

Opinions in the Federal Courts of Appeals were equally devoid of evidence that this Court had announced a general proportionality principle. Some evaluated "cruel and unusual punishment" claims without reference to *Weems*. . . . Others continued to echo (in dictum) variants of the dictum in *State v. Becker* [1892] to the effect that courts will not interfere with punishment unless it is "manifestly cruel and unusual," and cited *Weems* for the proposition that sentences imposed within the limits of a statute "ordinarily will not be regarded as cruel and unusual." . . . Not until more than half a century after *Weems* did the Circuit Courts begin performing proportionality analysis. Even then, some continued to state that "[a] sentence within the statutory limits is not cruel and unusual punishment" [*Page v. United States* (1972)].

Denying Prisoners Medical Attention Violates the Eighth Amendment

Thurgood Marshall

In the case of *Estelle v. Gamble* (1976), the Supreme Court determined that deliberate indifference to a prisoner's medical needs constitutes cruel and unusual punishment and is therefore prohibited. Prisoner J.W. Gamble was injured in prison in 1973 while unloading a bale of cotton from a truck. He received intermittent medical treatment that was, in his opinion, insufficient. The Supreme Court heard his case, and the majority opinion, by Thurgood Marshall, is excerpted here. The Court agreed that a denial of appropriate medical treatment would indeed cause needless pain and suffering and would be "inconsistent with contemporary standards of decency." The Court thereby concluded that indifference to a prisoner's medical needs would violate the Eighth Amendment. Ironically, however, it was determined that Gamble himself did not receive "deliberate indifference" to his medical condition. His case, while beneficial to other prisoners, did not directly benefit him. Thurgood Marshall served on the Supreme Court from 1967 to 1991.

According to the complaint, [prisoner J.W.] Gamble was injured on November 9, 1973, when a bale of cotton fell on him while he was unloading a truck. He continued to work but after four hours he became stiff and was granted a pass to the unit hospital. At the hospital a medical assistant, "Captain" Blunt, checked him for a hernia and sent him back

Thurgood Marshall, majority opinion, *Estelle v. Gamble,* 429 U.S. 97, 1976.

to his cell. Within two hours the pain became so intense that Gamble returned to the hospital where he was given pain pills by an inmate nurse and then was examined by a doctor. The following day, Gamble saw a Dr. Astone who diagnosed the injury as a lower back strain, prescribed Zactirin (a pain reliever) and Robaxin (a muscle relaxant), and placed respondent on "cell-pass, cell-feed" status for two days, allowing him to remain in his cell at all times except for showers. On November 12, Gamble again saw Dr. Astone who continued the medication and cell-pass, cell-feed for another seven days. He also ordered that respondent be moved from an upper to a lower bunk for one week, but the prison authorities did not comply with that directive. The following week, Gamble returned to Dr. Astone. The doctor continued the muscle relaxant but prescribed a new pain reliever, Febridyne, and placed respondent on cell-pass for seven days, permitting him to remain in his cell except for meals and showers. On November 26, respondent again saw Dr. Astone, who put respondent back on the original pain reliever for five days and continued the cell-pass for another week.

On December 3, despite Gamble's statement that his back hurt as much as it had the first day, Dr. Astone took him off cell-pass, thereby certifying him to be capable of light work. At the same time, Dr. Astone prescribed Febridyne for seven days. Gamble then went to a Major Muddox and told him that he was in too much pain to work. Muddox had respondent moved to "administrative segregation." On December 5, Gamble was taken before the prison disciplinary committee, apparently because of his refusal to work. When the committee heard his complaint of back pain and high blood pressure, it directed that he be seen by another doctor.

On December 6, respondent saw petitioner [Dr. Ralph] Gray, who performed a urinalysis, blood test, and blood pressure measurement. Dr. Gray prescribed the drug Ser-Ap-Es for the high blood pressure and more Febridyne for the back pain. The following week respondent again saw Dr. Gray, who continued the Ser-Ap-Es for an additional 30 days. The prescription was not filled for four days, however, because the staff lost it. Respondent went to the unit hospital twice more in December, both times he was seen by Captain Blunt, who prescribed Tiognolos (described as a muscle relaxant). For all of December, respondent remained in administrative segregation.

In early January, Gamble was told on two occasions that he would be sent to the "farm" if he did not return to work. He refused, nonetheless, claiming to be in too much pain. On January 7, 1974, he requested to go on sick call for his back pain and migraine headaches. After an initial refusal, he saw Captain Blunt who prescribed sodium salicylate (a pain reliever) for seven days and Ser-Ap-Es for 30 days. Respondent returned to Captain Blunt on January 17 and January 25, and received renewals of the pain reliever prescription both times. Throughout the month, respondent was kept in administrative segregation.

On January 31, Gamble was brought before the prison disciplinary committee for his refusal to work in early January. He told the committee that he could not work because of his severe back pain and his high blood pressure. Captain Blunt testified that Gamble was in "first class" medical condition. The committee, with no further medical examination or testimony, placed respondent in solitary confinement.

Four days later, on February 4, at 8 A.M., respondent asked to see a doctor for chest pains and "blank outs." It was not until 7:30 that night that a medical assistant examined him and ordered him hospitalized. The following day a Dr. Heaton performed an electrocardiogram; one day later respondent was placed on Quinidine for treatment of irregular cardiac rhythm and moved to administrative segregation. On February 7, respondent again experienced pain in his chest, left arm, and back and asked to see a doctor. The guards refused. He asked again the next day. The guards again refused. Finally, on February 9, he was allowed to see Dr. Heaton, who ordered the Quinidine continued for three more days. On February 11, he swore out his complaint.

The Elementary Principles of the Eighth Amendment

The gravamen of respondent's complaint is that petitioners have subjected him to cruel and unusual punishment in violation of the Eighth Amendment, made applicable to the States by the Fourteenth. We therefore base our evaluation of respondent's complaint on those Amendments and our decisions interpreting them.

The history of the constitutional prohibition of "cruel and unusual punishments" has been recounted at length in prior opinions of the Court and need not be repeated here. . . . Accordingly, this Court first applied the Eighth Amendment by comparing challenged methods of execution to concededly inhuman techniques of punishment. See *Wilkerson v. Utah* (1879) ("It is safe to affirm that punishments of torture . . . and all others in the same line of unnecessary cruelty, are forbidden by that amendment . . ."); *In re Kemmler* (1890) ("Punishments are cruel when they involve torture or a lingering death . . .").

Our more recent cases, however, have held that the Amendment proscribes more than physically barbarous punishments. The Amendment embodies "broad and idealistic concepts of dignity, civilized standards, humanity, and decency . . ." [*Jackson v. Bishop* (1968)] against which we must evaluate penal measures. Thus, we have held repugnant to the Eighth Amendment punishments which are incompatible with "the evolving standards of decency that mark the progress of a maturing society" [*Trop v. Dulles* (1958)] or which "involve the unnecessary and wanton infliction of pain" [*Gregg v. Georgia* (1976)]. . . .

These elementary principles establish the government's obligation to provide medical care for those whom it is punishing by incarceration. An inmate must rely on prison authorities to treat his medical needs; if the authorities fail to do so, those needs will not be met. In the worst cases, such a failure may actually produce physical "torture or a lingering death," *In re Kemmler*, . . . the evils of most immediate concern to the drafters of the Amendment. In less serious cases, denial of medical care may result in pain and suffering which no one suggests would serve any penological purpose. The infliction of such unnecessary suffering is inconsistent with contemporary standards of decency as manifested in modern legislation codifying the common-law view that "it is but just that the public be required to care for the prisoner, who cannot by reason of the deprivation of his liberty, care for himself."

Indifference to Prisoners' Medical Needs Violates the Eighth Amendment

We therefore conclude that deliberate indifference to serious medical needs of prisoners constitutes the "unnecessary and wanton infliction of pain" [*Gregg v. Georgia*] proscribed by the Eighth Amendment. This is true whether the indifference is manifested by prison doctors in their response to the prisoner's needs or by prison guards in intentionally denying or delaying access to medical care or intentionally interfering with the treatment once prescribed. Regardless of how evidenced, deliberate indifference to a prisoner's serious illness or injury states a cause of action. . . .

Not Every Complaint Constitutes Indifference

This conclusion does not mean, however, that every claim by a prisoner that he has not received adequate medical treatment states a violation of the Eighth Amendment. An accident, although it may produce added anguish, is not on that basis alone to be characterized as wanton infliction of unnecessary pain. In *Louisiana ex rel. Francis v. Resweber* [1947], for example, the Court concluded that it was not unconstitutional to force a prisoner to undergo a second effort to electrocute him after a mechanical malfunction had thwarted the first attempt. Writing for the plurality, Mr. Justice [Stanley] Reed reasoned that the second execution would not violate the Eighth Amendment because the first attempt was an "unforeseeable accident." Mr. Justice [Felix] Frankfurter's concurrence, based solely on the Due Process Clause of the Fourteenth Amendment, concluded that since the first attempt had failed because of "an innocent misadventure," the second would not be "'repugnant to the conscience of mankind,'" quoting *Palko v. Connecticut* [1937].

Similarly, in the medical context, an inadvertent failure to provide adequate medical care cannot be said to constitute "an unnecessary and wanton infliction of pain" or to be "repugnant to the conscience of mankind." Thus, a complaint that a physician has been negligent in diagnosing or treating a medical condition does not state a valid claim of medical mistreatment under the Eighth Amendment. Medical malpractice does not become a constitutional violation merely because the victim is a prisoner. In order to state a cognizable claim, a prisoner must allege acts or omissions sufficiently harmful to evidence deliberate indifference to serious medical needs. It is only such indifference that can offend "evolving standards of decency" in violation of the Eighth Amendment.

Gamble's Care Is Deemed Not Indifferent

Against this backdrop, we now consider whether respondent's complaint states a cognizable claim. The handwritten pro se document is to be liberally construed. As the Court unanimously held in *Haines v. Kerner* [1972], a pro se complaint, "however inartfully pleaded," must be held to "less stringent standards than formal pleadings drafted by lawyers" and can only be dismissed for failure to state a claim if it appears "'beyond doubt that the plaintiff can prove no set of facts in support of his claim which would entitle him to relief.'" quoting *Conley v. Gibson* (1957).

Even applying these liberal standards, however, Gamble's claims against Dr. Gray, both in his capacity as treating physician and as medical director of the Corrections Department, are not cognizable. . . . Gamble was seen by medical personnel on 17 occasions spanning a 3-month period: by Dr. Astone five times; by Dr. Gray twice; by Dr. Heaton three times; by an unidentified doctor and inmate nurse on the day of the injury; and by medical assistant Blunt six times. They treated his back injury, high blood pressure, and heart problems. Gamble has disclaimed any objection to the treatment provided for his high blood pressure and his heart problem; his complaint is "based solely on the lack of diagnosis and inadequate treatment of his back injury." . . . The doctors diagnosed his injury as a lower back strain and treated it with bed rest, muscle relaxants and pain relievers. Respondent contends that more should have been done by way of diagnosis and treatment, and suggests a number of options that were not pursued. The Court of Appeals agreed, stating: "Certainly an x-ray of (Gamble's) lower back might have been in order and other tests conducted that would have led to appropriate diagnosis and treatment for the daily pain and suffering he was experiencing." But the question whether an X-ray or additional diagnostic techniques or forms of treatment is indicated is a classic example of a matter for medical judgment. A medical decision not to order an X-ray, or like measures, does not represent cruel and unusual punishment. At most it is medical malpractice, and as such the proper forum is the state court under the Texas Tort Claims Act. The Court of Appeals was in error in holding that the alleged insufficiency of the medical treatment required reversal and remand. That portion of the judgment of the District Court should have been affirmed.

The Court of Appeals focused primarily on the alleged actions of the doctors, and did not separately consider whether the allegations against the Director of the Department of Corrections, [W.J.] Estelle [Jr.], and the warden of the prison, [H.H.] Husbands, stated a cause of action. Although we reverse the judgment as to the medical director, we remand the case to the Court of Appeals to allow it an opportunity to consider, in conformity with this opinion, whether a cause of action has been stated against the other prison officials.

Solitary Confinement Might Be Cruel and Unusual Punishment

Regan Good

"Supermax" facilities are prisons that keep inmates totally isolated for twenty-three hours a day. Such sensory deprivation often leads to serious mental illness, according to critics, and is therefore cruel and unusual. In the following selection, Regan Good describes efforts to challenge the constitutionality of these institutions. Ironically, Good notes, those who do develop mental illnesses are often "rewarded" with an end to their solitary confinement. Healthy inmates—those who do not destabilize—have no legal recourse under the Eighth Amendment. Regan Good is a writer based in New York City.

The billboard at the east entrance to the remote rural village of Tamms, Illinois, reads "Tamms: The First Super Max," and below, in lowercase letters, "a good place to live." Inmates at Tamms, who live in a kind of state-sanctioned suspended animation, would tend to disagree. Confined to their cells, alone, twenty-three hours a day, inmates eat, sleep, defecate, urinate, read and write (if they are able), watch TV or listen to the radio (if they are allowed) in the same 8-by-12 cell, often for years on end. The monotony, sensory deprivation and mandated idleness of supermax confinement is especially torturous for inmates who have—or who develop during incarceration, as many do—a serious mental illness. It is this fact that forms the crux of the lawsuit filed against the prison in 1999 by Jean Maclean Snyder, a lawyer at the

MacArthur Justice Center at the University of Chicago Law School. Snyder charges that the treatment of mentally ill prisoners at Tamms amounts to cruel and unusual punishment, a violation of their Eighth Amendment rights.

The lawsuit represents four plaintiffs, three of whom have attempted suicide. The MacArthur suit, like other challenges to supermaxes, was filed on behalf of the mentally ill among the Tamms population, but these suits are, in Snyder's words, "a surrogate for generalized legal challenges to supermaxes," which rarely prevail in court.

In what has been interpreted as a direct reaction to the MacArthur Center's lawsuit, Tamms opened a special mental health wing, called "J-Pod," in February 2000. This high-surveillance unit receives inmates who are broken enough, according to Illinois Department of Corrections standards, to be relieved of continual isolation—in essence, Tamms created a special unit to combat the effects of its policies, rather than consider reforming the regime. Here inmates are allowed daily contact with mental health staff and some interaction with other inmates. Even in J-Pod inmates must "earn" their way out of Tamms by correcting their behavior. But as Snyder points out, many mentally ill inmates can't "behave," by definition. And for those stuck in solitary confinement, she adds, "there is nothing to be good at, there is no behavior allowed." (Since Tamms opened in 1998, only fourteen men have "graduated" from the supermax and been sent back to lesser-security prisons.)

Craig Haney, a national expert on the mental health of US prisoners and a professor of psychology at the University of California, Santa Cruz, has watched as supermaxes have spread unchecked across the nation. Haney was one of the original witnesses in a 1994 federal district court lawsuit against California's notorious Pelican Bay isolation unit. The decision in that case stated that the mentally ill could not and should not be made to endure supermax conditions. Haney remembers the day he and a colleague first toured the facility. "We drove most of the two hours back to the airport without saying a word. It was as though we had seen the face of the future of American corrections, and it was terrifying.

They had come as close as humanly possible to creating a long-term storage container for people."

The Current Supermax Status

Inmates are not sentenced to supermax; they supposedly "earn" their way in through violent behavior, gang affiliation and an accumulation of disciplinary infractions in other prisons. The corrections sector insists these prisons work to keep both guards and other inmates safe, and historically, courts have deferred to their opinion. Currently, thirty to thirty-five states have supermax facilities, either existing as freestanding prisons or blocks of isolation cells in lesser-security prisons. At any given moment, there are about 25,000 people in long-term solitary confinement in the United States.

Because they provide J-Pod for their most desperate inmates, Tamms officials believe the prison is both escape- and litigation-proof. After three years in operation, Tamms remains about half-full, currently holding 265 inmates, though it has room for 500. The Illinois Department of Corrections says this is evidence of its careful and judicious selection; critics say it is evidence of gross overbuilding.

Under current Eighth Amendment jurisprudence, healthy inmates have no meaningful legal recourse. Attempts like Snyder's to file challenges on behalf of seriously mentally ill inmates have better prospects. Snyder, who is now waiting for a trial date, has ample evidence of the brutal conditions and paucity of treatment facing her mentally ill defendants (although the Southern District of Illinois is a difficult place for inmates to get a fair hearing). A recent decision in Boscobel, Wisconsin, made it clear that the state must keep the mentally ill out of its supermax; another recent case in Florida was settled, with the main concession being, once again, that mentally ill inmates have no place in supermax confinement. Still, in each of these cases the basic supermax paradigm was reaffirmed. So the "normal resilience" inmates will remain in their cells, keeping track of time by the sound of the metal meal carts clanking down the wings. Ironically, their best hope for transfer or legal redress may be their own psychological collapse.

Three Strikes and You're In

George F. Will

California's "three strikes" law mandates that offenders who commit three felonies must receive an automatic life sentence. In March 2003 the Supreme Court ruled that the law was not unconstitutional. The case involved two persons, Gary Ewing and Leandro Andrade, who had committed relatively petty crimes but received life sentences. They argued that their sentences were grossly disproportionate to their crimes and were therefore cruel and unusual. The Court disagreed and upheld their sentences. In the following selection George F. Will expresses his support for the ruling. Will is an ABC News commentator, a Pulitzer Prize winner, and the author of a syndicated column that appears in more than 450 newspapers. Will has been a contributing editor to *Newsweek* since 1976.

If being dumb were a crime, Gary Ewing and Leandro Andrade would be Al Capone and Don Corleone. And if "possibly misguided" or "arguably unfair" were synonyms for "unconstitutional," perhaps the Supreme Court should have struck down the sentences imposed on Ewing and Andrade under California's "three strikes" law.

But they are not synonyms. So the Supreme Court last week rightly refused, in two 5-4 rulings, to prevent California from punishing Ewing and Andrade with the "three strikes and you're out" law passed in 1994, under which someone convicted for any felony after two previous convictions for "serious" or "violent" felonies can be incarcerated for a long spell.

Someone like Ewing, who in 2000 was on parole from a nine-year prison term when he tried to walk out of the pro shop at a Los Angeles country club with three $399 golf clubs concealed in his pants leg. Or someone like Andrade, a heroin addict stealing to support his habit, who in 1995 was stopped by security personnel at a California Kmart as he tried to steal five videotapes worth $84.70, and who 14 days later was stopped by security personnel as he tried to walk out of another Kmart with four videotapes worth $68.84 tucked in the waistband of his pants.

Ewing has been convicted of battery, thefts, burglaries, and drug-related offenses in a series of crimes running back to 1984, when he was 22. Andrade, too, had a series of convictions, including some for residential burglaries, which count as "serious" felonies under the three-strikes law. Ewing's golf-club theft earned him a sentence of 25 years to life. Andrade's two videotape thefts earned him 50 years without possibility of parole.

Twenty-six states have some version of such a law. California acquired its nearly a decade ago. In 1993 the California Legislature considered a three-strikes bill, intended to deter or incapacitate repeat offenders by mandating "an indeterminate term of life imprisonment" for recidivists. When that bill was defeated, public anger fueled a drive to get such a law on the November 1994 ballot.

While petitions to achieve that were circulating, 12-year-old Polly Klaas was kidnapped and murdered by a man with a long criminal record that included two kidnapping convictions. Had he served his full 16-year sentence, rather than just half of it, for his most recent conviction (for kidnapping, assault and burglary), Polly would be alive. The three-strikes proposal qualified for the ballot faster than any initiative in California history. It won by a 72 percent majority.

Under it, prosecutors can choose to treat a recidivist's misdemeanor as a "third strike." More than 7,000 persons are serving long three-strikes sentences in California. The third offenses committed by 344 of those inmates were petty thefts.

This is a story of discretion, and the restriction of it. The criminal-justice system is lubricated by prosecutorial discretion: without plea bargains, the system would collapse. But the three-strikes law, a product of understandable public fury about irresponsibly—in the Polly Klaas case, lethally—lenient sentencing, limits discretion in sentencing.

Whether three-strikes laws go too far in removing mind—case-by-case judgment—from certain criminal-justice cases is a matter of opinion about social policy. Which is why the Ewing and Andrade cases illuminate today's fierce arguments about proper judging.

Ewing and Andrade said their sentences are unconstitutional because of the Eighth Amendment's proscription of "cruel and unusual punishments." The four most liberal Supreme Court justices—Breyer, Ginsburg, Stevens and Souter—agreed.

They argued that there can be such "gross" disproportionality between the pettiness of a crime and the severity of a sentence that the sentence is "cruel and unusual." But this is inherently standardless, more a visceral reaction than a judicial judgment. Furthermore, they focused on the "triggering" crime, not on the preceding pattern of crimes. Given the fact of federalism, and the federalist ethic of broad respect for states' differing policy choices, it is difficult to see the pertinence of the dissenters' data showing that most other states would impose lesser punishments on criminals similar to Ewing and Andrade who commit similar crimes.

The five more conservative justices—Kennedy, O'Connor, Rehnquist, Scalia, Thomas—opted for a modest judicial role. O'Connor, a former Arizona state legislator who wrote the opinions in both cases, said California law reflects "a rational legislative judgment, entitled to deference." And: "We do not sit as a 'superlegislature' to second-guess these policy choices."

By the way, in affirming the constitutionality of the Andrade sentence, the Supreme Court overruled the hyperliberal and frequently reversed Ninth Circuit. Yes, that is that merry band of jurisprudential improvisers who recently discovered that the words "under God" in the Pledge of Allegiance constitute an unconstitutional "establishment of religion." That discovery will be reversed.

Punishment in Schools Is Not Prohibited by the Eighth Amendment

Patricia H. Hinchey

The Supreme Court ruled in 1977 that Eighth Amendment privileges do not extend into the realm of schools. Thus, schools have the right to inflict corporal punishments, such as paddlings, if they so choose. In the following selection Patricia H. Hinchey explores individual cases of harsh corporal punishment and discusses the fact that the United States is one of only a handful of nations that still exercises corporal punishment on a regular basis. Patricia H. Hinchey is an associate professor of education at Penn State University.

F or some time now, I have been talking to practitioners about corporal punishment in schools, especially middle and high schools. Practitioner responses to my questions about the legal status of paddling and other physical discipline in their states have fallen into two categories: surprise that I would ask about the subject as if practices such as paddling still existed anywhere, and surprise that I would ask about the topic as if paddling weren't common in every school in the country. Most teachers appear to assume that the status of corporal punishment in their own school or state is a national standard—a perception that is far from contemporary reality. The following quiz will help readers determine the reliability of their own perceptions relating to this topic:

Patricia H. Hinchey, "Corporal Punishment Legalities, Realities, and Implications," *Clearing House,* vol. 76, January/February 2003, pp. 127–31. Copyright © 2003 by the Helen Dwight Reid Educational Foundation. Reproduced with permission of the Helen Dwight Reid Educational Foundation, published by Heldref Publications, 1319 18th St. NW, Washington, DC, 20036-1802.

Corporal Punishment: True or False?

- The issue of corporal punishment has reached the United States Supreme Court, which has upheld the practice as constitutional.

- Military personnel and criminals have the right to due process before corporal punishment can be imposed; as a matter of federal law, schoolchildren, on the contrary, do not.

- Early in his term in office, President George W. Bush promoted legislation that would protect educators who had beaten children from lawsuits. Both teachers' unions, the NEA (National Education Association) and the NIT (National Federation of Teachers), opposed this legislation, intended to protect their members.

- Researchers have demonstrated that corporal punishment can constitute a form of sexual abuse.

However unlikely it may seem to many readers, the answer in every case is "true."

The Eighth Amendment Protects Criminals, Not Schoolchildren

The Supreme Court case that now provides the foundation for corporal punishment policies is *Ingraham v. Wright* (1977). Two students, James Ingraham and Roosevelt Andrews, suffered severe paddlings in their Florida junior high school that left Ingraham needing medical attention for severe pain and bruising and Andrews unable in one instance to use his arm for a week. Their suit argued that the paddlings were unconstitutional, in violation of the Eighth Amendment's prohibition of cruel and unusual punishment and also of the Fourteenth Amendment's guarantee of due process. The Court, however, rejected both arguments. Because corporal punishment has long been common among parents and school officials alike, the Court found, it could not be classified as "cruel and unusual." Moreover, the Court found that the Eighth Amendment is intended to protect criminals, not schoolchildren, and that children who suffered severe punishment could gain redress by prosecuting officials on such charges as assault and battery, a recourse thought to be sufficient protection for children.

Although many parents and students have indeed sought legal redress for severe beatings, they rarely win in court—making it especially difficult to understand why President Bush has supported a legislative effort to prohibit lawsuits against educators. Courts have found in favor of schools and teachers even when the punishment they imposed included paddling a nine-year-old seven times within half an hour; sticking a straight pin into a student's arm; confining children in closets and other small, dark spaces; slamming them into walls; and stuffing and/or taping children's mouths. Parents have also been dismayed to lose cases filed after a child was paddled without parental permission. Unless a school chooses to abide by parental wishes, parents in states where corporal punishment is legal can protect their children from beatings only by removing them from schools that employ paddling.

Sometimes the offenses against children are so egregious that it seems unbelievable that courts would find for schools and against the family, but it routinely happens. For example, one seventeen-year-old female, who was both an honor student and a senior with no prior record of misbehavior, skipped school. This young adult was forced to bend over a desk and submit to several blows inflicted by an adult male coach whom she had trusted until the incident. For the girl, consequences included not only the physical pain of the beating, but also menstrual hemorrhaging and long lasting emotional trauma. Despite arguments that the case involved not only physical but also sexual abuse, the school won the case. In fact, over and over again corporal punishment has been linked to sexual abuse, although many state legislators who could outlaw the practice apparently remain unmoved by such arguments.

Nor is any special consideration offered to students with disabilities, for whom courts have upheld paddling, isolation, and mouth taping as punishments. In one case, a disabled student was forced to do exercise so rigorous that it led to his death. Rather than finding such incidents a cause for restraining corporal punishment, legislators have blithely moved forward toward solidifying educators' legal right to impose physical punishment on students with disabilities. In June 2001, a bill enabling discipline of the disabled was introduced by U.S. Senator Jeff Sessions of Alabama and passed the United States Senate.

As the following examples illustrate, courts rarely punish abusive educators in states that allow corporal punishment.

America Refuses to Restrict Corporal Punishment

It is perhaps telling that the United States is one of two countries worldwide that have not yet ratified the Convention on the Rights of the Child, adopted by the United Nations General Assembly in November 1989. The other is Somalia. The document calls for multiple protections of the human rights of children, including the right to be protected from violence.

As other countries of the world move toward greater and greater protection of their children, with Northern Ireland and Scotland strengthening laws against corporal punishment in 2001, the United States retains its dubious distinction of being one of very few developed countries whose national policy allows corporal punishment in schools. Over one hundred organizations joined forces to call this fact to national attention in a widely publicized letter to the president of the United States: "Throughout the developed, industrial world, and in many developing nations, the use of corporal punishment against schoolchildren is forbidden. No European country permits the practice." Organizations signing the letter included the American Academy of Pediatrics, the National Congress of Parents and Teachers Association, the National Mental Health Association, the American Psychological Association, the American Association of Physicians for Human Rights, the National Association of School Psychologists, the American School Counselor Association, and the National Committee for Prevention of Child Abuse.

However, the organizations' plea that the president "instruct the Secretary of the U.S. Department of Education to take expeditious and forceful action to deny federal assistance to any school, school district, or other educational

entity that authorizes the use of corporal punishment" has
fallen on deaf ears. The effort has also been undermined both
by President Bush's support for legislation protecting those
who beat children and by Senator Sessions's efforts to make
sure that all children are equally subject to such beatings. A
[2001] *Houston Chronicle* story reported the case of several
Canadian parents who moved to Ohio and Indiana to escape
the Canadian law prohibiting the use of such objects as pad-
dles, sticks, and belts to inflict punishment on children. In
Ohio and Indiana, parents (and others) are free to strike children with such instruments.

For those concerned about the physical safety and mental
health of children, the good news is that legislators in
twenty-seven states and the District of Columbia have
heeded the research and advice of pediatricians, parents, educators, and others and have passed state laws prohibiting
corporal punishment in schools. However, that leaves children in nearly half of all states still subject to the abuses of
corporal punishment with little or no practical means of prevention or redress. . . .

Although defenders of corporal punishment argue that
few incidents are excessive, a review of news reports indicates otherwise—and that the extreme cases are sufficiently
horrifying to justify exclusion of corporal punishment, whatever the rate of incidence.

The Realities of Corporal Punishment in the United States

All of the following incidents were reported in newspapers
during 2001. In the context of cases with results as severe as
death, some cases seem almost trivial by comparison. Still, it
is likely that most parents would be greatly upset by the actions of a California teacher who, despite a ban on corporal
punishment, taped a first-grader's mouth shut and threatened to tie her up; and of an Arizona teacher who tried to force
a sixth-grader to chew gum already chewed by others and
saved in a jar for the purposes of this punishment. Such bodily indignities, however, are the least of what a child may suffer in school, as other reported incidents nationwide reveal.

An Oklahoma Christian school teacher struck a 12-year-old with a 3-foot long dowel because he was passing notes in class and inflicted bruises that hospital doctors characterized as "severe." A parent in Louisiana was unsuccessful in filing a criminal action against an assistant principal who broke a paddle on a 13-year-old. A parochial school director in Florida was arrested after using a wooden board to paddle an 8-year-old, leaving a mark some 4 inches wide and 6 inches long and welts as high as a quarter of an inch. In another Florida incident, a dean at an elementary school was found guilty of misdemeanor battery for excessively beating an 8-year-old; he was required to take an anger-management course and subsequently returned to his role as school leader—although after this incident, the school did ban corporal punishment. In Michigan, another state where corporal punishment is legally restricted, a 15-year-old freshman football player did not return to school for weeks after he received 10 blows with a paddle that eventually cracked. Some six or seven other players were also hit, one approximately 12 or 13 times. In Tennessee, a school employee faced criminal charges after hitting a 15-year-old in the arm with a baseball bat.

A national antispanking group called for a civil rights audit of students in Mobile, Alabama, because black children in recent years have received 65 to 70 percent of all paddlings there, although they make up slightly less than half of all students. Statistics also indicated that on the whole, for the 1998–99 school year, 73 percent of paddlings administered statewide in Alabama were to the black students who make up only 41 percent of its total school population.

If all reports related to religious schools and alternative "boot-camp" type schools were included, this list would be much longer.

The Origins of the American Bill of Rights

The U.S. Constitution as it was originally created and submitted to the colonies for ratification in 1787 did not include
what we now call the Bill of Rights. This omission was the
cause of much controversy as Americans debated whether to
accept the new Constitution and the new federal government
it created. One of the main concerns voiced by opponents of
the document was that it lacked a detailed listing of guarantees of certain fundamental individual rights. These critics
did not succeed in preventing the Constitution's ratification,
but were in large part responsible for the existence of the
Bill of Rights.

In 1787 the United States consisted of thirteen former
British colonies that had been loosely bound since 1781 by
the Articles of Confederation. Since declaring their independence from Great Britain in 1776, the former colonies
had established their own colonial governments and constitutions, eight of which had bills of rights written into them.
One of the most influential was Virginia's Declaration of
Rights. Drafted largely by planter and legislator George
Mason in 1776, the seventeen-point document combined
philosophical declarations of natural rights with specific limitations on the powers of government. It served as a model
for other state constitutions.

The sources for these declarations of rights included English law traditions dating back to the 1215 Magna Carta
and the 1689 English Bill of Rights—two historic documents
that provided specific legal guarantees of the "true, ancient,
and indubitable rights and liberties of the people" of England. Other legal sources included the colonies' original charters, which declared that colonists should have the same
"privileges, franchises, and immunities" that they would if
they lived in England. The ideas concerning natural rights

developed by John Locke and other English philosophers were also influential. Some of these concepts of rights had been cited in the Declaration of Independence to justify the American Revolution.

Unlike the state constitutions, the Articles of Confederation, which served as the national constitution from 1781 to 1788, lacked a bill of rights. Because the national government under the Articles of Confederation had little authority by design, most people believed it posed little threat to civil liberties, rendering a bill of rights unnecessary. However, many influential leaders criticized the very weakness of the national government for creating its own problems; it did not create an effective system for conducting a coherent foreign policy, settling disputes between states, printing money, and coping with internal unrest.

It was against this backdrop that American political leaders convened in Philadelphia in May 1787 with the stated intent to amend the Articles of Confederation. Four months later the Philadelphia Convention, going beyond its original mandate, created a whole new Constitution with a stronger national government. But while the new Constitution included a few provisions protecting certain civil liberties, it did not include any language similar to Virginia's Declaration of Rights. Mason, one of the delegates in Philadelphia, refused to sign the document. He listed his objections in an essay that began:

> There is no Declaration of Rights, and the Laws of the general government being paramount to the laws and constitution of the several States, the Declaration of Rights in the separate States are no security.

Mason's essay was one of hundreds of pamphlets and other writings produced as the colonists debated whether to ratify the new Constitution (nine of the thirteen colonies had to officially ratify the Constitution for it to go into effect). The supporters of the newly drafted Constitution became known as Federalists, while the loosely organized group of opponents were called Antifederalists. Antifederalists opposed the new Constitution for several reasons. They believed the presidency would create a monarchy, Congress would not be truly representative of the people, and state governments would be endangered. However, the argument that proved most effective was that the new document lacked a bill of rights and thereby threatened Americans with the loss of cherished individual liberties. Federalists realized that to gain the support of key states such as New York and Virginia, they needed to pledge to offer amendments to the Constitution that would be added immediately after its ratification. Indeed, it was not until this promise was made that the requisite number of colonies ratified the document. Massachusetts, Virginia, South Carolina, New Hampshire, and New York all included amendment recommendations as part of their decisions to ratify.

One of the leading Federalists, James Madison of Virginia, who was elected to the first Congress to convene under the new Constitution, took the lead in drafting the promised amendments. Under the process provided for in the Constitution, amendments needed to be passed by both the Senate and House of Representatives and then ratified by three-fourths of the states. Madison sifted through the suggestions provided by the states and drew upon the Virginia Declaration of Rights and other state documents in composing twelve amendments, which he introduced to Congress in September 1789. "If they are incorporated into the constitution," he argued in a speech introducing his proposed amendments,

> Independent tribunals of justice will consider themselves in a peculiar manner the guardians of those rights; they will be an impenetrable bulwark against every assumption of power in the legislative or executive; they will be naturally led to resist every encroachment upon rights expressly stipulated for in the constitution by the declaration of rights.

After debate and some changes to Madison's original proposals, Congress approved the twelve amendments and sent them to the states for ratification. Two amendments were not ratified; the remaining ten became known as the Bill of Rights. Their ratification by the states was completed on December 15, 1791.

Supreme Court Cases Involving the Freedom from Cruel and Unusual Punishment

1867

Pervear v. Commonwealth of Massachusetts
Pervear was the first test of the Eighth Amendment before the Supreme Court. The defendant was convicted for illegally selling and keeping intoxicating liquors. His fine of fifty dollars and three months imprisonment was determined to be constitutional, as it was "the usual mode adopted in many, perhaps, all of the States."

1878

Wilkerson v. Utah
The Supreme Court decided that death by firing squad for the offense of first-degree murder was not unconstitutional. The Court determined that the method was not "unusual," as Utah had a long history of such punishment.

1890

In re Kemmler
The first use of the electric chair was challenged. The Court determined that while the method was indeed unusual, it was *not* cruel, and was thereby allowable.

1910

Weems v. United States
The Supreme Court ruled that the Eighth Amendment applied not only to punishments considered cruel and unusual by the framers of the Constitution in 1789 (a historical interpretation), but also to punishments considered cruel and unusual according to society's evolving standards.

1958

Trop v. Dulles
The Supreme Court determined that divestiture of citizenship, or the revoking of a person's right to be a citizen, was constitutionally forbidden as a penalty more cruel and "more primitive than torture."

1972

Furman v. Georgia
Capital punishment was judged unconstitutional based on discrepancies in its administration with regard to race and other factors.

1976

Estelle v. Gamble
The Court determined that deliberate indifference to a prisoner's medical needs is cruel and unusual, and thereby prohibited.

Gregg v. Georgia
The Supreme Court overturned its ruling in *Furman*, stating that the death penalty itself was not unconstitutional, but the methods used in seeking its applicability had been. Once measures were put into place to ensure that the death penalty was being administered to all criminals in a fair and balanced manner, the penalty itself was no longer considered cruel and unusual.

1983

Solem v. Helm
A split Court found that a life sentence without the possibility of parole for a seventh nonviolent felony was cruel and unusual, and thereby unconstitutional. The Court stated in this ruling that some degree of proportionality, or matching the harshness of the punishment to the gravity of the crime, must exist.

1991

Harmelin v. Michigan
The Supreme Court declared that the Eighth Amendment includes no proportionality guarantee, meaning that there is no guarantee that harsher crimes will indeed receive harsher sentences or that similar crimes will receive similar sentences. This in effect weakened the ruling in *Solem*.

2002

Atkins v. Virginia
The execution of mentally challenged offenders was declared cruel and unusual.

2003

Ewing v. California
The Supreme Court upheld California's strict "three strikes law," under which three felony offenses result in a nonnegotiable life sentence. Gary Ewing, the defendant, received such a sentence after stealing $399 worth of golf clubs. His sentence was upheld, and the three strikes law still stands.

Books

Akhil Reed Amar, *The Bill of Rights: Creation and Reconstruction*. New Haven, CT: Yale University Press, 2000.

Robert M. Baird and Stuart E. Rosenbaum, eds., *Punishment and the Death Penalty: The Current Debate*. Amherst, NY: Prometheus, 1995.

Stuart Banner, *The Death Penalty: An American History*. Cambridge, MA: Harvard University Press, 2002.

Hugo Adam Bedau, *The Death Penalty in America: Current Controversies*. New York: Oxford University Press, 1997.

Hugo Adam Bedau and Paul G. Cassell, *Debating the Death Penalty: Should America Have Capital Punishment? The Experts on Both Sides Make Their Best Case*. New York: Oxford University Press, 2004.

Elliott Currie, *Crime and Punishment in America*. New York: Metropolitan, 1998.

James R. Eisenberg, *Law, Psychology, and Death Penalty Litigation*. Sarasota, FL: Professional Resource, 2004.

Jack Kevorkian, *Prescription Medicide: The Goodness of Planned Death*. Buffalo, NY: Prometheus, 1993.

Barry Latzer, *Death Penalty Cases*. 2nd ed. Burlington, MA: Butterworth-Heinemann/Elsevier Science, 2002.

Leonard W. Levy, *Origins of the Bill of Rights*. New Haven, CT: Yale Nota Bene, 2001.

Linda R. Monk, *The Words We Live By: Your Annotated Guide to the Constitution*. New York: Stonesong/Hyperion, 2003.

Jack N. Rakove, *Original Meanings: Politics and Ideas in the Making of the Constitution*. New York: First Vintage/Random House, 1996.

Mark A. Siegel, Donna R. Plesser, and Nancy R. Jacobs, eds., *Capital Punishment, Cruel and Unusual?* Plano, TX: Information Aids, 1986.

Scott Turow, *Ultimate Punishment: A Lawyer's Reflections on Dealing with the Death Penalty.* New York: Farrar, Straus & Giroux, 2003.

John R. Vile, *A Companion to the United States Constitution and Its Amendments.* 2nd ed. Westport, CT: Praeger, 1997.

Web Sites

The American Civil Liberties Union, www.aclu.org/Death Penalty/DeathPenaltyMain.cfm. The ACLU's mission is to preserve the protections guaranteed by the Constitution. This link leads to information regarding its stance on the death penalty.

The Death Penalty Information Center, www.deathpenalty info.org. The Death Penalty Information Center is a non-profit organization serving the media and the public with analysis and information on issues concerning capital punishment.

FindLaw for Legal Professionals, http://caselaw.lp.findlaw. com/data/constitution/amendment08. FindLaw provides legal resources via the Internet for legal professionals, businesses, students, and individuals. This link leads to information on the Eighth Amendment.

Justice For All, www.prodeathpenalty.com. Founded in 1993, Justice For All is a victims' rights group advocating change in the criminal justice system.

The Juvenile Justice Center, www.abanet.org/crimjust/juvjus/home.html. The Juvenile Justice Center is a program of the American Bar Association. Information regarding capital punishment for juveniles may be found on this Web site.